LEGACY OVER EGO

15 Laws to Flip the Game and Leave Your Mark

Bryan Code Name Genesis

Legacy Over Ego: 15 Laws to Flip the Game and Leave Your Mark

By Bryan Jones (Bryan Code Name Genesis)

Copyright © 2025 by Bryan Jones

All rights reserved. No part of this publication may be reproduced, stored in a retrieval system, or transmitted in any form or by any means—electronic, mechanical, photocopying, recording, or otherwise—without prior written permission of the publisher, except for brief quotations in articles or reviews.

ISBN (Hardcover): 979-8-9923395-1-2

ISBN (Paperback): 979-8-9923395-4-3

ISBN (eBook): 979-8-9923395-3-6

Cover design by **Arslan Shani**

Published by **Bryan Jones Publishing**

Printed in the United States

Disclaimer: This book is based on the author's personal experiences and opinions. Neither the author nor the publisher shall be held liable for any damages arising from the use or misuse of the information contained herein.

For more information and updates, visit: Bryzentech.com

DEDICATION

To my children, Thank you.

Thank you for your patience with my long lessons and for enduring my stern challenges, even when it felt like too much. Every word I've spoken, every lesson I've tried to teach, and every boundary I've held was rooted in love—a love so deep it shaped the man I've become.

You are my greatest inspiration, my unshakable reason, and the foundation of my courage. There is no me without you. You are the ones who made me brave enough to write this book, to share my truths, and to leave behind a legacy worthy of you.

I love you beyond words, time, and anything this world could ever measure.

This book is for you.

Forever yours,

Pop

PREFACE

This isn't a book for the weak. This isn't a guide for the helpless, the hopeful, or the ones sitting around waiting for someone to save them. You won't find fairy tales in these pages. There's no prince, no savior, no lifeboat. There's only you.

And that's the most powerful thing you could ever realize.

You see, the world has lied to you. It told you to look outside yourself for answers—search for the right job, the right partner, and the right moment to make your move. It told you to wait for permission, to seek validation, to follow a path someone else carved. But the truth is, the only map you'll ever need is buried in your chest. Your solutions aren't out there—they're locked inside of you, waiting for you to turn the key.

You were born with magic in your bones. Every answer you're searching for is written in the ink of your blood. But society has done a damn good job of convincing you otherwise. It trained you to doubt your instincts, question your power, and believe in limits that don't even exist. You were programmed to forget that you are the source.

This book is here to wake you up. To shake you out of the dream you've been living and drop you into the raw, undeniable reality of your power.

We're going to dive deep—beneath the masks you wear for the world, beyond the excuses you've told yourself, and into the darkest corners of your soul. That's where the game begins. That's where the laws are written. That's where you'll find the version of yourself who doesn't just survive but dominates.

Understand this: life is a game, but it's not fair. It never was. The board is rigged, the players are ruthless, and the rules are hidden in plain sight. But none of that matters. Because once you unlock yourself, once you learn to maneuver with precision and purpose, no obstacle can stop you.

This book isn't just words. It's a mirror. A master key. Each page is designed to strip away your illusions, confront your demons, and arm you with the laws you need to move through this world like a force of nature.

But let me warn you now: this isn't easy. It's raw. It's uncomfortable. It will make you question everything you thought you knew. Some of you will close this book halfway through because the truth is too much. But those who finish it will walk away transformed.

The world doesn't owe you anything, and no one's coming to save you. But that's the best news you'll ever hear, because it means you don't have to wait. You are your own savior, your own master, your own alchemist.

This book will challenge you to step into the arena and claim your place—not with permission, but with purpose, not with compromise, but with conviction. These 15 **laws** aren't just lessons; they're weapons to dismantle what's held you back and build an unshakable foundation.

The question isn't whether you can do it. It's whether you'll choose to.

Because at the end of these pages, you won't just understand the code—you'll become it. You'll write your story in the ink of your victories and live it with the fire of a legacy in the making.

The only question left is: Are you ready to stop playing small and start playing to win?

If you're still here, if the fire inside you is burning brighter, let's begin.

Who I Am and Why You're Here

Let me start with this: I'm not supposed to be here.

I wasn't born into privilege or handed a silver spoon. There were no safety nets, no golden tickets, no roadmaps to success waiting for me. I was born into chaos. My mother passed away when I was just eight years old—a loss so deep it cracked my world wide open. My father? A ghost living in the shadows of addiction. The family I knew? Torn apart, scattered like ash on the wind, leaving me to navigate a world that didn't give a damn whether I rose or fell.

And let's be real—I fell. Hard.

By the time most kids were dreaming of their futures, I was staring down a reality that felt more like a nightmare. The streets became my teacher, and pain was the only lesson plan. I didn't walk into adulthood—I stumbled, tripped, and crashed, making every mistake a man can make and inventing some new ones along the way. I skipped the detours and sprinted straight into hell with open arms.

No direction. No guidance. No safety net. Just a royal screw-up on a crash course with rock bottom.

You want to talk about failure? I didn't get my GED until I was 30. Thirty. Let that sink in. By the time most people were climbing career ladders, building families, and chasing dreams, I was clawing my way out of a pit so deep it felt like daylight was a myth. But here's the truth they don't tell you: rock bottom isn't the end—it's the beginning.

Rock bottom strips away all the lies you've been telling yourself. It burns away the ego, the excuses, and the illusions you've clung to. It's where you meet the raw, unfiltered version of yourself—the you that can either give up or rise. And me? I chose to rise.

But rising isn't clean. It's messy. It's painful. It costs you everything.

When I finally started to climb out of that pit, I thought the battle was over. I was wrong. The world didn't cheer for me—it turned on me. The higher I climbed, the more I felt the knives in my back. Friends I thought were family betrayed me. People I trusted twisted my vulnerabilities into weapons. They didn't care about my scars or the battles I fought to get here; they just wanted the crown I was building for myself.

And I wasn't innocent either. I hurt people. I burned bridges. I let my pain bleed into the lives of those who tried to love me. I became the very thing I hated—angry, reckless, destructive. The cycle of betrayal didn't start with them, and it didn't end with me.

For three years, I lived in seclusion—trapped in a vortex of my pain, fear, and self-doubt. I was alone, afraid, drowning in my tears. It was a death of sorts, but not just of the life I knew; it was the death of who I was.

I had to kill the old versions of me—the man who blamed the world, the man who let fear dictate his choices, the man who allowed the opinions of others to shape his destiny. Those versions had to die for me to live.

And in the fire of that loneliness, that pain, that self-destruction, a new man emerged.

Forged in flames, I became something different. Stronger. Wiser. Unbreakable. I learned that no one outside of me could define my fate, write my story, or tell me what I could or couldn't do. I learned to trust the fire in my chest, the voice in my gut, and the unshakable truth that I am the source of my power. I'm not here because the world let me win. I'm here because I refused to lose.

So now, let me ask you this: what's holding you back? What excuse are you clutching like a life raft? Is it your past? Your mistakes? Your circumstances? Let me be clear—I had all those too, and they didn't stop me.

You're here because you're tired. Tired of running, tired of blaming, tired of pretending you don't have what it takes. Deep down, you know it's time to stop hiding behind the lies you've told yourself. You know it's time to stop waiting for the world to change and start changing yourself.

Here's the raw truth: no one's coming to save you. Not now, not ever. The sooner you accept that, the sooner you'll realize the only savior you've ever needed is staring back at you in the mirror. You are the hero of this story. You've always been the hero.

But heroes aren't handed greatness. They fight for it.

I'm not here to coddle you. I'm not here to sugarcoat your path or hold your hand. I'm here to hand you the keys to the game, the codes to the matrix, and the 15 laws that will teach you how to rise, how to fight, how to dominate. What you do with them is entirely up to you.

So, I'll leave you with one question before you turn the page: are you ready to stop running? Because once you start this journey, there's no turning back.

Welcome to the fire. Welcome to the truth.

Now, let's see what you're made of.

TABLE OF CONTENTS

Dedication v

Preface vi

Chapter 1: The Master Key: Unlock Yourself, Unlock the Game 2

Chapter 2: The Art of War with Yourself: Conquer Within, Conquer All 10

Chapter 3: The Shadow Players Not Everyone Deserves to Walk in Your Light 17

Chapter 4: The Illusion of the Plug: Stop Chasing Power— You Are the Source 24

Chapter 5: The Game is Rigged, Play Anyway Break the Illusion, Master the Board 31

Chapter 6: The Mirror Never Lies Face Yourself, Own Yourself, Free Yourself 39

Chapter 7: The Storm That Shapes Us 47

Chapter 8: The Illusion of Time Master the Clock, Command Your Destiny 56

Chapter 9: The Law of Seasons Honor the Cycle, Respect the Harvest 65

Chapter 10: The Masks We Wear Drop the Disguise, Reclaim Your Power 74

Chapter 11: The Ladder and the Bridge Break Free, Build Your Ascent 83

Chapter 12: The Power of Silence Speak Less, Move More 91

Chapter 13: The Phoenix Principle Burn to Rise, Break to Become 100

Chapter 14: The Weight of the Crown The Price of Power, The Test of Legacy 109

Chapter 15: Legacy Over Ego Build Forever, Not for Applause 118

Why I Wrote This Book 125

CHAPTER 1

The Master Key: Unlock Yourself, Unlock the Game

The Voice of Truth

Before the world was formed, the Master Key was forged. It was not given to the strong or the swift. It was placed deep within every soul, hidden like a treasure in the heart of chaos, waiting to be discovered. And now, the time has come for you to claim what was always yours. But understand this: you cannot unlock the world until you unlock yourself.

You stand at a door, pounding and pleading for it to open. You've spent years blaming the lock, cursing the door, and begging for the key. But here is the truth: the key has always been in your hand.

The Story of Rashad: A Soul Lost in Shadow

Rashad sank into the secondhand couch in his cramped apartment, the city's neon glow filtering through the blinds. Outside, distant sirens and muffled laughter drifted upward, but inside, it was all silence— heavy, oppressive silence that pressed against him like a weight. The place still held echoes of his girlfriend's voice, the slam of the front door, and that final, lingering question: *When are you going to look at yourself?*

At twenty-nine, Rashad couldn't remember the last time he felt any real direction. Months turned into years, each one blurring into the next. Promotions passed him by, relationships soured, and opportunities dried up. He told himself the system was rigged. The world was cold. People like him weren't meant to catch a break. He had a thousand excuses, polished and ready whenever life refused to open its doors.

Tonight, though, the apartment's silence refused to comfort him. Usually, he'd lose himself online, scrolling, comparing, blaming. But Veronica's words still hung in the air, and he couldn't outrun them.

Her absence felt like a hole in the room's fabric. He tried to swallow the lump in his throat, but it lodged there— a knot of regret and fear. He closed his eyes and pressed his palms together as if praying —or maybe just bracing himself.

For too long, he'd seen life as a series of locked doors. No one would give him the key. He had cursed and pounded his fists on those doors, convinced he deserved better. But here he was, alone in a dingy apartment, no closer to anything he truly wanted. *Was it really the world's fault?*

He opened his eyes and caught a faint reflection in the dark TV screen: his own shape, blurred and hollow. Something in that distorted figure unsettled him. He realized he was afraid—afraid of what he might see if he looked too closely. Afraid of the truths he'd buried under layers of resentment and denial.

Then he heard it—not a sound from the street, not a knock on the door, but a voice inside, calm and steady, cutting through the silence. It wasn't loud, but it was unmistakable.

Stop running, Rashad.

He lurched upright, heart pounding. It had been so quiet a moment ago, and now this voice seemed to fill every corner of the room. It felt ancient and patient, as though it had waited years for him to finally listen.

You think the world locked you out, but you've been holding the key all along.

Rashad's breath caught. He wanted to argue, to protest, but the words sank into his chest with a gravity he couldn't ignore. They carried a truth that unsettled him far more than the locked doors ever had.

He rose slowly, his legs unsteady, and stepped toward the bathroom. He flicked on the harsh fluorescent light and stared into the mirror. He rarely looked at himself this closely—looked. Dark circles were carved beneath his eyes. His shoulders slumped. His face wore the weight of years spent blaming everyone else.

"Who are you?" he asked, voice barely above a whisper. His reflection offered no answer, but that voice inside him spoke again, soft but firm:

You are more than your failures, more than your fear. Everything you need is already within you, buried beneath your excuses and doubt.

Tears welled in his eyes. He felt exposed, vulnerable, as if someone had stripped him of all his defenses. He understood, in that moment, that no door would open until he acknowledged who he truly was— and who he could become. The problem had never been the door. It was that he didn't know himself, didn't trust himself, and had never dared to confront the mess inside.

He leaned closer to the mirror, tears slipping down his cheeks. He saw not just the tired man he'd become, but the possibility of someone stronger, wiser. Someone who could face the truth and forge his own key. The fear that once felt like a prison guard now felt like a guidepost, pointing toward the work he'd avoided.

Rashad backed away from the sink, heart pounding with a strange new rhythm—one that whispered of change rather than dread. He returned to the living room, feeling lighter, though nothing in the room had changed. He didn't have all the answers, but he had a starting point: himself.

Not perfect. Not fixed. But ready.

Ready to face the fears he'd fled. Ready to acknowledge that he was the common denominator in all those locked doors. Ready to dig through the layers of ego and illusion to find the key that had been in his hand all along.

The Voice of the Source

The voice wasn't loud, but it was undeniable. It wasn't harsh, yet it carried the weight of truth.

"Stop running, Rashad." He froze.

"You think the world locked you out, but you've been holding the key all along. The problem isn't the door—it's that you don't know who you are. How can you open what you haven't unlocked within yourself?"

Rashad felt his chest tighten. The voice wasn't condemning him; it was awakening him.

"The fear you feel is not your enemy—it's your guide. The pain you carry is not a curse—it's your teacher. But you cannot rise while clinging to who you've been. The man you were must die so the man you're meant to be can live."

Tears streamed down Rashad's face. For the first time, he realized he wasn't fighting the world. He was fighting himself.

Rashad stood and walked to the bathroom. He flicked on the light and stared at the mirror. His reflection stared back — hollow, tired. "Who are you?" he whispered.

The question hung in the air, heavy with truth.

The voice returned, stronger this time:

"You are more than your failures—more than your fears. You are the source. Everything you need is already within you, but you've buried it beneath excuses, distractions, and doubt. It's time to dig it out.

It's time to unlock the door."

Rashad didn't know how long he stood there, but by the time he left the bathroom, he felt different.

Not fixed. Not perfect. But ready. Ready to stop running. Ready to face himself.

The Law of the Master Key

The voice spoke one last time, and it sounded like thunder in his soul:

"Listen carefully: The Master Key is self-awareness. Without it, every door remains locked. You will wander aimlessly, chasing shadows, until you recognize the truth of who you are.

Self-awareness is the foundation. It is the map, the compass, and the key. But it is not easy. To wield it, you must confront your deepest fears, slay your ego, and dismantle every lie you've built your life around. Only then will you be free."

How to Forge the Master Key

1. *Face Your Fears (The Truth Will Set You Free)*

"Fear is not your enemy—it is your invitation to grow."

The voice reminded Rashad that fear only controls you when you avoid it. To unlock the door, you must walk through the fire.

Action Step: Write down the three fears you avoid most. Read them aloud. Then ask yourself, *"What is fear trying to teach me?"*

2. *Kill the Ego (Humble Yourself Before Truth)*

"Ego is the armor of the insecure. Strip it off and let truth sharpen you."

Rashad realized his pride was his prison. Ego had convinced him to run from feedback to avoid admitting when he was wrong.

Action Step: Identify one area where your ego is holding you back. Apologize to someone you've hurt or ask someone for feedback without defending yourself.

3. *Audit Your Patterns (Break the Chains)*

"The patterns you refuse to break become the chains that bind you."

The voice revealed that Rashad's habits—procrastination, avoidance, and distraction—were the real locks on his potential.

Action Step: Reflect on your last three failures. Write down the patterns that led to them. Then, commit to one small change this week to break the cycle.

4. Trust the Process (Growth is Painful but Worth It)

"Growth is not comfort. Growth is death and rebirth. Trust the fire—it's forging you."

Rashad wanted results overnight, but the voice reminded him that unlocking himself was a process, not a shortcut.

Action Step: Start a daily ritual of reflection. Whether it's journaling, meditation, or prayer, commit to 10 minutes a day to connect with yourself.

The Final Word

"The Master Key is yours to forge — no one can do it for you. The door will remain closed until you unlock yourself. The world is waiting for you to rise, but first, you must meet yourself. You must face the mirror, confront the truth, and claim the power that has always been within you. The question is not whether you have the key; The question is: are you ready to use it?" Rashad wasn't perfect, but he took the first step. And that's where his transformation began.

Now, it's your turn. Will you unlock yourself, or will you keep pounding on the door?

The key is in your hand. What will you do with it?

CHAPTER 2

The Art of War with Yourself: Conquer Within, Conquer All

The Voice of Truth

Before the first battle was fought on Earth, the greatest war raged within. This war has no soldiers, no banners, no weapons you can hold. Its battlefield is your mind. Its enemy? You.

This is the art of war with yourself—a battle you must fight every day. And understand this: no external victory will ever last if you lose this war.

You want to build something great? You want to claim your throne? Then first, you must conquer the chaos within.

Vanessa's dreams were bigger than the small town that tried to contain her. She wanted to write a book that would touch strangers' hearts, to start a business built from her vision, and to see places far beyond the horizon of familiar streets. In her mind, she pictured a life filled with purpose and freedom, where she could wake each morning and feel the pulse of destiny in her veins.

But reality looked different. Each time she tried to begin, she froze. She'd sit at her laptop, meaning to write the first sentence, but somehow end up scrolling through social media until her eyes blurred.

She'd sketch out plans for her business on Pinterest boards but never muster the courage to send a single email or make one phone call. She'd browse travel blogs, saving destinations she swore she'd visit "one day," yet never reached for her credit card to actually book the flight.

Days piled into weeks, weeks slid into months, and Vanessa found herself paralyzed. Her mind had become a war zone: on one side stood her dreams—bold, shining with possibility— on the other loomed the dark silhouette of doubts she could not silence. *What if you fail? Who are you to think you can do this? You're not ready yet.* These whispers gnawed at her confidence until making every step forward felt like stepping off a cliff.

Late one night, after yet another wasted evening, Vanessa sat on the floor of her tiny bedroom, the quiet hum of her phone and the distant hum of passing cars were the only interruptions to the silence. The soft glow of her lamp fell across her notebook, still blank despite her grand intentions. Tears slid down her cheeks, warm and bitter.

"Why can't I just do it?" she whispered into the empty air, her voice cracking with frustration and shame.

She didn't expect an answer. Yet in that stillness, something stirred inside her. It wasn't loud or forceful, but steady and certain, like the echo of a distant drum reverberating in her chest. At first, she thought it was her imagination, but the words she heard were too clear to ignore.

The Voice of the Source

"Vanessa, your war is not with the world. It is with yourself." Her breath caught.

"You are fighting battles that do not exist. Procrastination, self-doubt, fear—they are shadows, illusions created by your mind. They are not real. But their power comes from your belief in them. You've handed them the keys to your life. It's time to take them back."

Vanessa sat up, wiping her tears. The voice was calm yet commanding, as though it carried an ancient truth she had always known yet somehow forgotten.

"Understand this: You are both the prisoner and the warden. The chains that bind you are the ones you forge with your thoughts. To win this war, you must master the art of war with yourself."

The Law of Internal Conquest

The voice continued:

"The enemy within is not invincible. Procrastination is fear in disguise. Self-doubt is the echo of old wounds. They are paper tigers, roaring to keep you small. But you have a weapon they cannot withstand: awareness paired with action.

Victory begins the moment you refuse to let your thoughts control you. You are not your doubts. You are not your fears. You are the commander of your soul, the warrior of your own mind. To conquer within is to conquer all."

How to Wage War with Yourself

1. *Recognize the Enemy (Name the Shadows)*

    "The first step in any battle is identifying the enemy. Call your shadows by their name."

Vanessa realized that her procrastination wasn't laziness—it was fear. Fear of failure, fear of success, fear of the unknown.

Action Step: Write down the habits that are sabotaging you—procrastination, self-doubt, perfectionism. Ask yourself, "What fear is hiding behind this habit?"

2. *Break the Illusion (Take Back Control)*

"Fear thrives on illusion. Break the illusion, and the enemy loses its power." The voice reminded Vanessa that each time she delayed action, she fed the illusion of fear. The solution was simple: move. Even the smallest step would start to shatter the lie that she couldn't act.

Action Step: Choose one small action related to your goal and do it immediately. Not tomorrow. Not in an hour. Now.

3. *Build the Ritual of Victory (Discipline is Your Sword)*

"Discipline is the weapon of the warrior. Without it, battles are lost before they begin."

Vanessa understood that her scattered efforts were an invitation to chaos. She needed a daily ritual— small, consistent actions to gain momentum.

Action Step: Design a daily ritual. For Vanessa, it could be writing 500 words each morning before touching her phone. What will yours be?

4. **Reframe the Battlefield (Make Fear Your Ally)**

"Fear is not your enemy—it is your compass. Follow it, and it will lead you to growth." Vanessa learned to stop running from fear. Instead, she would ask what fear was trying to protect her from and what it was pointing her toward.

Action Step: When fear arises, write down what it's telling you. Then flip the script: What opportunity is hidden in this fear?

Esoteric Insight: The Power of Inner Conquest

"You are the warrior, the battlefield, and the victory. The battle is not to defeat yourself but to master yourself. For when the mind is conquered, the world bows in surrender."

The Final Word

The voice concluded:

"Vanessa, the war will not end overnight. This is a daily battle, one you will fight until your last breath.

But every time you choose action over fear, discipline over chaos, courage over doubt, you win.

The art of war with yourself is the art of self-mastery. It is not easy, but it is worth it. For when you conquer within, there is no battle you cannot face."

Vanessa rose from the floor, determination replacing her tears. She opened her notebook and wrote the first sentence of her book. It was far from perfect, but it existed—and in that moment, she won her first battle.

Now, it's your turn. What shadow are you fighting? What fear is holding you back? The war is waiting, and the victory is yours to claim.

The question is: *Will you fight?*

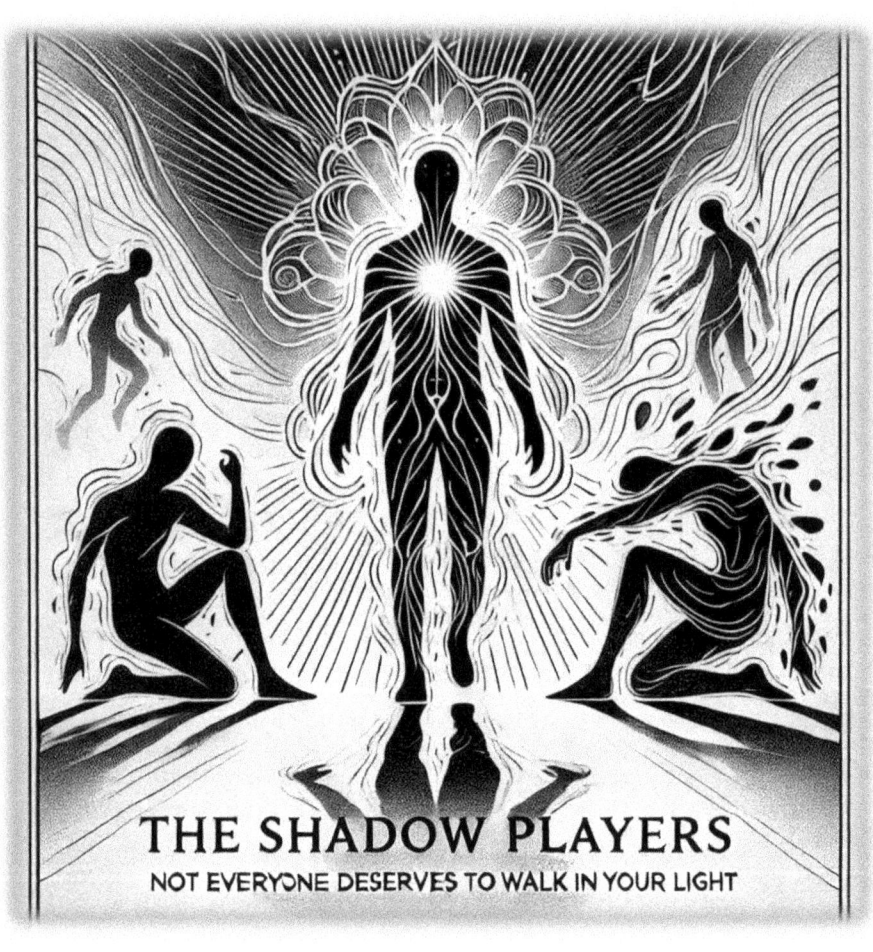

CHAPTER 3

The Shadow Players Not Everyone Deserves to Walk in Your Light

The Voice of Truth

The brighter your light, the darker the shadows that follow. They will sit at your table, smile in your face, and toast to your success—all while sharpening the knife for your back. They will call themselves friends, brothers, and sisters—but watch their hands, not their words. Some are not here to help you build; they are here to break you down.

Understand this: the Shadow Players have no power except the power you give them. Your first mistake is ignoring what your spirit already knows. Your second mistake? Leaving your light unguarded.

This is where you learn to see, to discern, and to move with the wisdom of one who knows the cost of betrayal but refuses to dim their light.

The Story: Malik and the Weight of Betrayal

Malik had always believed in loyalty. He learned it as a boy, running through cracked sidewalks with Dre, Marcus, and Reggie—three faces he never imagined turning against him. They'd grown up scraping by on the same streets, dreaming of something better. Nights spent on corner stoops imagining futures built on more than hustle and hope had forged what Malik thought was an unbreakable bond.

By the age of twenty-six, he had accomplished what few from his neighborhood managed: he had turned his ambition into a real business. It wasn't just for him; it was meant for all of them. With careful planning and relentless drive, Malik secured contracts, expanded his client list, and created opportunities that could lift his whole crew. He brought Dre, Marcus, and Reggie into every deal, gave them roles, and offered room to grow, believing that if he rose, they'd rise too.

But beneath the surface, envy festered. At first, Malik brushed off the small signs. Dre would scoff at his plans, calling them "pipe dreams" and masking thinly veiled barbs as jokes. Marcus, the smooth talker, never quite followed through on his promises, yet always stepped forward when it was time to share credit. Reggie, the quiet one Malik trusted most, became secretive, ending phone calls whenever Malik entered the room. Malik tried to ignore the uneasy churn in his gut.

When a key deal slipped through his fingers because someone leaked details to a competitor, Malik felt a chill in his bones. He wanted to blame bad luck, but the evidence pointed too clearly toward Reggie. Still, he hesitated, refusing to believe that someone who had started shoulder-to-shoulder with him would sabotage his future.

The final blow came late one night after a meeting ran long. As Malik stepped outside a downtown bar, he caught Dre and Marcus talking in the alley's half-light. He pressed himself against the brick wall, heart pounding even before he understood why.

"Malik thinks he's the boss of us," Dre sneered. "He wouldn't be sh*t without us. I'm just waiting for him to blow up so I can get my cut and bounce."

Marcus laughed softly, "All that talk of loyalty—whatever. Once I get mine, I'm gone. No need to stick around when I can do better on my own."

Their voices cut Malik like a blade. These were the men he'd trusted with his life, the ones he'd sworn would always have his back. He felt the air leave his lungs as if he'd been punched. Every sacrifice he'd made, every opportunity he'd shared, had been met not with gratitude, but with greed. They never celebrated his light; they only waited for a chance to steal it.

Later that night, Malik sat alone in his office, head in his hands. A strangled mix of rage and hurt twisted inside him. He'd built something beautiful and tried to bring his brothers along, but their hearts were filled with envy, not unity. He wondered how he could've missed the signs if he had listened to his instincts instead of ignoring that uneasy churn. If only he had honored the subtle warnings…

The world outside was quiet, the dim glow of streetlights stretching shadows across his desk. He felt the weight of betrayal pressed on him—heavy, personal. In that silence, a voice rose from within him, stronger than his anger, clearer than his pain.

The Voice of the Source

"Malik, why are you surprised? Did you think your light would go unnoticed? The brighter you shine, the more shadows gather to consume you.

The Shadow Players are drawn to your success, not to celebrate it— they come to dim it."

The voice grew louder, more insistent:

"Understand this: betrayal is not a reflection of you—it is a revelation of them. Not everyone who starts the journey with you is meant to finish it. Not everyone who stands beside you deserves a place in your circle. Your mistake was ignoring the signs. Your mistake was giving your trust where it was not earned."

The Law of Discernment

"The Shadow Players will not announce themselves, but they will reveal themselves if you listen, if you watch, and if you trust what you feel.

Discernment is your weapon. Learn to separate the loyal from the envious, the allies from the opportunists. Protect your energy as if it were sacred —because it is. Do not give your light to those who would only use it to cast shadows."

How to Identify and Defeat the Shadow Players 1.

1. Listen to Their Words (Envy Has a Voice)

"The tongue will always betray the heart. Pay attention to how they speak about your success." Dre's "jokes" were Malik's first warning, but he ignored them. Envy always slips through in words, often disguised as humor or criticism.

Action Step: Reflect on how people react to your wins. Do they celebrate genuinely, or do they throw subtle shade?

2. Observe Their Actions (Loyalty is Shown, Not Spoken)

"Words are easy. Watch their actions—loyalty is proven in the doing."

Marcus's empty promises were a clear sign he was only in it for himself.

Action Step: Write down three instances when someone in your circle showed up for you without expecting anything in return. If you can't think of any, it's time to reassess.

3. Trust Your Intuition (Your Spirit Knows)

"Your gut is a divine compass. Stop ignoring the signals."

Malik's instincts warned him about Reggie, but blind loyalty kept him from seeing the truth.

Action Step: Think of one person who feels "off" in your circle. Write down the signs you've ignored.

4. Protect Your Light (Move in Silence)

"The less they know, the less they can destroy. Let your moves speak louder than your words." Not everyone needs to know your plans. Shadow Players thrive on information. Silence is your shield.

Action Step: Choose one major goal and commit to keeping it private until it's accomplished.

Esoteric Insight: Light Draws Shadows

"The brighter you shine, the more shadows you cast. Do not dim your light to make others comfortable. Instead, illuminate the shadows so they cannot hide. Let your light be your protection and your weapon."

The Final Word

The voice concluded:

"Malik, betrayal is painful, but it is also a gift. It reveals the truth of those around you. Use this truth to move wisely, protect your energy, and surround yourself with those who build, not those who destroy.

The Shadow Players will always be there, but they cannot harm what they cannot touch. Your light is too powerful to be consumed by shadows."

Malik understood what he had to do. Without rage, without drama, he stepped back from Dre, Marcus, and Reggie. He shed their presence as one sheds a heavy coat in summer. In time, he rebuilt his circle with those who truly believed in him —people who reflected his growth instead of resenting it.

Now it's your turn. Who in your life is a Shadow Player? What signs have you ignored? The time for excuses is over. Protect your energy. Move with wisdom. Let your light shine, unbothered by the shadows.

The question is: *Will you let them steal your light, or will you guard it with everything you have?*

CHAPTER 4

The Illusion of the Plug: Stop Chasing Power—You Are the Source

The Voice of Truth

You've been chasing shadows, begging for access, and waiting for someone to hand you the key. You tell yourself that only if you could just find the right person, the right connection, the right plug, everything would fall into place.

But hear this truth: the plug you seek does not exist.

You are the source. Everything you need to build, grow, and rise is already within you. The world has taught you to beg for crumbs when you were born to bake the bread. The time for waiting is over. It's time to stop chasing and start creating.

The Story: Jada and the Endless Chase

Jada grew up in a cramped apartment on the east side of Detroit, where ambition was both a currency and a burden. From the time she could hold a pencil, she sketched dresses and jackets in the margins of her schoolwork, imagining a future filled with vibrant colors and bold lines.

Her mother worked long hours cleaning hotel rooms, and Jada would sit on the bed at night, tracing new designs under the glow of a single lamp, dreaming of the day her clothes would light up a runway.

She was restless and resourceful. In high school, Jada customized thrifted jackets for classmates, transforming their old denim into statement pieces that turned heads in hallways and at house parties.

Everyone told her she had talent, and that she was going places. But no one offered a roadmap. No one said, "Here's how you turn talent into a brand." Detroit's hustle surrounded her, but it also swallowed people whole. She believed that she could leapfrog the struggle if she could find the right connection—someone who already had a platform.

So she chased the plug.

First came Andre, the boutique owner with a decent online following. Jada offered to promote his store, styling outfits and taking photos for free, hoping he'd return the favor. He eagerly accepted her work, but when Jada gently asked for a mention or a referral, Andre brushed her off with a dismissive smile. "Keep grinding," he said, shrugging. "Maybe someday." His tone made her feel small, as if her efforts were a minor convenience rather than a valuable contribution.

Next came Tasha, a stylist who boasted connections to local influencers. Tasha promised Jada introductions— "the right people"—if Jada kept producing custom pieces at no cost. Eager for that break, Jada poured hours into sewing late at night, hand-stitching details that made each garment unique. Clients raved about the pieces. Yet when it came time for credit, Tasha took the spotlight, acting as if the work was hers alone. Jada swallowed her pride, telling herself each freebie was an investment in her future. But the promised doors never opened.

Months blurred into years. Jada's savings thinned as she funneled money into materials, photography, and shipping. She watched as others she admired launched small lines online, gathering loyal followings. She felt like a satellite orbiting success, always close but never landing. The rejections and brush-offs started to chip away at her spirit. Each broken promise felt like a hand pushing her back into the shadows.

One night, after a particularly stinging rejection from Tasha—who laughed off Jada's request to be tagged in a client post—Jada slumped onto her couch. She held her sketchbook in her lap, flipping through pages of dreams that had yet to see the light of day. Tears blurred her vision.

"What am I doing wrong?" she whispered into the silence of her living room. She had thought working for others, impressing them, and waiting patiently would grant her a ticket into their world. Instead, she was left with nothing but exhaustion and self-doubt.

The apartment felt too quiet, the lamplight too stark. In that hush, a voice rose within her—not loud, but unmistakably firm and true.

The Voice of the Source

"Jada, why are you begging for what is already yours?"

Her heart skipped. The voice continued, calm but unyielding:

"You've spent years chasing connections, thinking they hold the power. But the truth is, you are the source. You are the creator. The power you've been searching for is already in your hands. You don't need permission to build your dream. Stop chasing the plug. Start becoming the plug."

Jada froze, the words cutting through her haze of doubt. She realized every time she'd bowed her head, begging for a morsel of recognition, she'd handed over her power. Every time she waited for someone else's nod, she delayed her own destiny.

"Listen to me," the voice said. "Every shortcut costs double in the end. Every person you've chased has shown you the truth—they are not the source of your success. You are. Stop waiting for someone to give you a seat at their table. Build your own table."

The Law of Self-Reliance

"The universe rewards builders, not beggars. Stop looking for someone to save you. The only savior you need is within."

Jada realized she had been acting as if her potential required someone else's blessing. In truth, her skills were refined, her vision clear, and her talent undeniable. She already had the tools to start—on her own terms.

How to Stop Chasing and Start Building?

1. Reclaim Your Power (Stop Begging for Crumbs)

"When you chase others, you give them your power. Reclaim it."

Jada saw how every plea for a mention or a favor had drained her energy and self-worth. She vowed to end that cycle.

Action Step: Identify one area where you've been waiting for permission—whether it's launching a project, asking for a promotion, or pursuing a dream. Take one bold action today to move forward on your own.

2. Build Your Foundation (Start with What You Have)

"You don't need perfect conditions. Start with what's in your hands."

Jada inventoried her assets: her sewing machine, leftover fabric, and social media accounts. Everything she needed to start selling her designs directly was already within her reach.

Action Step: List three assets you already have—skills, tools, connections—and create a plan to use them to build your dream.

3. Shift Your Mindset (You Are the Plug)

"The plug you seek is an illusion. You are the source."

Jada realized waiting for a gatekeeper was a mindset trap. She resolved to act as the center of her own universe, creating gravity rather than orbiting someone else's world.

Action Step: Every morning, write down one thing you can do to invest in yourself, whether it's learning a skill, networking authentically, or producing work that reflects your vision.

4. Move with Purpose (Build, Don't Chase)

"Your energy is sacred. Invest it in creation, not desperation."

That very night, Jada took photos of three new original pieces. Instead of pitching them to someone else, she posted them online herself, with a caption that claimed her power: "I don't need permission. This is just the beginning."

Action Step: Set a goal for what you want to create or achieve in the next 30 days. Take consistent steps daily to bring it to life.

Esoteric Insight: You Are the Source

"The power you've been seeking is not out there. It is within you. Every tool you need to succeed is already in your hands. The world may try to convince you that you need permission, but the truth is, the only approval you need is your own."

The Final Word

The voice concluded:

"Jada, the world is filled with illusion. The plug, the connection, the shortcut—they are all traps designed to keep you small. Do not fall for them. Rise above them.

Stop asking for permission to shine. Build your light so bright that no one can ignore it. Stop chasing crumbs when you were born to bake the bread. You are the source. Act like it."

Jada closed her sketchbook, tears of frustration replaced by fierce determination. She would no longer waste time waiting at doors that refused to open. Instead, she'd build her own door, craft her own path, and let others see her brilliance on her terms.

Days later, as her designs gained traction, messages started rolling in—people asking where they could buy her work, small shops offering to feature her pieces. The same individuals who once overlooked her now sought her out. But Jada no longer craved their approval. She finally understood: her destiny was in her own hands.

Now it's your turn.

What are you waiting for? What permission are you begging for? The time for chasing is over. The time for building has begun.

***The question is:** Will you keep running in circles, or will you finally create the path forward?*

CHAPTER 5

The Game is Rigged, Play Anyway
Break the Illusion, Master the Board

The Voice of Truth

The game was never built for you.

It was designed in rooms you'll never enter by men who will never mention your name. The rules are invisible, the players are untouchable, and the goalposts move every time you get close. They want you to believe their power is absolute. They want you to think they've ascended to godhood, that their thrones were earned, and their success ordained.

But hear me now: they are frauds.

Their thrones are built on the backs of the unseen. Their rules exist to keep you chasing scraps. Their power thrives on your belief that they're untouchable. But the truth is, their power is paper-thin, their rules are a lie, and their greatest fear is you waking up.

The game is rigged. But the board is still yours to flip.

The Story: Chris and the House of Cards

Chris came from a family that believed hard work could solve anything. His parents, first-generation immigrants, had taught him that diligence was a key that opened any door. For most of his life, he trusted that formula. He worked two grueling jobs—managing a warehouse by day and driving deliveries by night. With every paycheck saved, every hour of sleep sacrificed, he pictured the truck he'd buy and the small fleet he'd someday own. He believed the system would reward him if he worked harder and longer.

But by the time he was twenty-eight, Chris began to see the cracks in that promise. The banks didn't care about his spotless credit and careful planning; they demanded collateral he didn't have. The smallbusiness grants he applied for turned him away with polite form letters, telling him to try again next year. The faces behind the counters and desks smiled professionally while they shut door after door. Meanwhile, Chris watched others—men who spoke in vague riddles, flashed designer suits, and name-dropped elusive connections—glide through the same doors he found locked.

He told himself he just needed a foot in. Someone who understood the game and could show him the ropes. That's how he ended up at a glitzy networking event, feeling out of place in his off-the-rack blazer. Everywhere he looked, men boasted about "conquering markets" and "leveraging assets," their laughter echoing over expensive cocktails. Chris hovered at the fringes, hoping to catch a stray invitation or a kind word.

That's when he met Derrick Blake. Derrick stood at the center of a cluster of admirers, wearing a suit that cost more than Chris made in a month and a watch that glittered under the chandelier light. He had a way of making promises sound like prophecies. "I can help you,

Chris," he said, pulling him aside. "You've got the hustle. You just need the right guidance. Stick with me, and I'll show you how to win."

Desperation is a powerful drug. Chris wanted to believe Derrick had the key. He scraped together $5,000 he couldn't afford to lose—his emergency fund, his truck down-payment savings—and handed it over. For months, Derrick dangled webinars and "exclusive" meetups in front of Chris like carrots on a string. He teased insider knowledge but served only platitudes. Every time Chris asked for something concrete, Derrick would say, "Keep grinding. Trust the process." That process led nowhere, just a hall of mirrors reflecting Chris's hopes back at him until they felt hollow.

One evening, after another pointless session, Chris parked his car on a dark street and stared at his nearly empty bank account on his phone. The realization hit him: Derrick never had any "secret keys" or "inside tips." He was a hustler selling dreams to strivers like Chris—people who labored under the illusion that someone else had the secret formula.

Chris felt rage rising in his throat—rage at Derrick for lying, at himself for trusting, and at the entire system that allowed men like Derrick to thrive. He slammed the steering wheel, heart pounding. How had he fallen for this? He worked too hard and sacrificed too much to be played like this.

That's when the voice came—not from outside, but from somewhere deep and undeniable inside him.

The Voice of the Source

"Chris, why are you chasing shadows? Do you think their power is real? The game is rigged, but the players you worship are not gods— they are pretenders. They sell illusions because they fear you will wake up and see the truth."

Chris's pulse steadied. He listened, shame melting into understanding.

"Their power only exists because you gave it to them. They don't hold the key. You do. You've been playing by their rules, running on their treadmill, waiting for their permission to rise. Stop. The system wasn't built for you to win, but that doesn't mean you can't."

The voice intensified, each word forging new clarity in Chris's mind: "The board is set against you, but it is not unbreakable. The rules are not sacred—they are tools. Learn them, bend them, rewrite them. The moment you stop asking for a seat at their table and start building your own, the game changes."

The Law of Strategic Play

"The game is not fair, but it can be mastered. The rules are hidden in plain sight, waiting for you to see them. The power they flaunt is not theirs to keep. The board belongs to the one who learns to play smarter, not harder."

Chris understood now. He'd been so obsessed with finding someone to unlock the game for him that he missed the fact he could carve out his own lane. He'd allowed the illusion of their superiority to blind him to his own capability.

How to Dominate a Rigged Game

1. Accept Reality (*The Game is Stacked*)

"Stop expecting fairness in a rigged world. Acceptance is the first move toward mastery." Chris realized he'd wasted energy raging against the unfairness. Now he would focus on outsmarting it.

Action Step: Write down three ways the system is stacked against you. Then write three ways you can maneuver through or around these obstacles.

2. *Expose the Illusion (They Are Not Gods)*

"The ones at the top are not invincible—they are manipulators, thriving on your belief in their power."

He saw that Derrick's supposed influence was a cheap trick. Others like him operated on bluff and bluster.

Action Step: Reflect on who you've been chasing for approval or access. Ask yourself, "What do they truly have that I can't create for myself?"

3. *Learn the Codes (Master the System)*

"The rigged game is not flawless. Its weakness is its arrogance. Study it, and you'll find its cracks."

Instead of complaining about barriers, Chris vowed to find alternative funding sources, community partnerships, and niche markets ignored by the big players.

Action Step: Research one unconventional method to bypass traditional barriers—community funding, peer-to-peer loans, or niche markets.

4. *Build Your Own Board (Create, Don't Chase)*

"Stop begging for a seat at their table. Build your own table. Their power fades when you create your own lane."

Chris reached out to a local mechanic who owned an idle truck. They struck a deal, sharing profits and responsibilities. Without begging anyone's permission, Chris created a path to move loads and start his dream operation.

Action Step: Identify one area where you can stop relying on external approval and start creating your own system— whether it's a side hustle, a community, or a skillset.

Esoteric Insight: Rewrite the Rules

"The game thrives on your obedience. But you were not born to obey. You were born to disrupt, to ascend, to master the board. The moment you stop chasing their power and start building your own, their game no longer matters."

Chris finally understood his potential was never theirs to grant or deny. He didn't need Derrick or anyone like him. He could use his own ingenuity, his own resources, to craft a route around the barricades. The rigged board would not define him; he would define it.

The Final Word

The voice concluded:

"Chris, the game is rigged, but it is not absolute. The players at the top fear you. They fear your hunger, your vision, your ability to see through their illusion.

The question is not whether you can win. The question is whether you will stop playing by their rules and start making your own. The board is waiting. The pieces are in your hands.

Will you move, or will you let the game play you?"

Chris wiped the frustration from his face. He would no longer chase frauds like Derrick. Instead, he would study the system's weak points, gather allies who shared his vision, and build something unshakeable.

With each strategic move he made, the once-impenetrable world began to bend to his will.

Now it's your turn.

Who or what have you been chasing? What illusion have you believed? The time for waiting is over.

The time for mastery has begun.

The question is: Will you rewrite the rules, or will you remain a pawn in their game?

CHAPTER 6

The Mirror Never Lies Face Yourself, Own Yourself, Free Yourself

The Voice of Truth

The world taught you to point fingers.

It told you the problem is always *"out there."* It whispered excuses in your ear: *"It's their fault." "The system is broken." "Life isn't fair."* And while you raged against everything outside of you, the truth sat silently, waiting for you to turn inward.

The mirror doesn't care about your excuses. It doesn't flinch at your anger, your fear, or your blame. It only shows you one thing: the unfiltered truth.

Radical accountability isn't punishment—it's liberation. The moment you stop running from yourself and face the reflection, the chains fall off. The time for lies, denial, and deflection is over. It's time to meet the only person responsible for your life: *you.*

The Story: Dante and the Echo of Excuses

Dante learned early how to shift blame. Growing up, he watched his father curse the world for his lost promotions and swear that their neighbors got lucky breaks he never did. Dante's mother sighed quietly behind him, folding laundry, never contradicting the bitterness that hung in their cramped apartment.

As a teenager, Dante adopted the same habit of externalizing everything. If the teacher was tough, it was the teacher's fault he struggled. If he lost a game, the ref was biased.

Now, at thirty-four, Dante's life looked nothing like the future he once imagined. He was broke, single, and stuck in a dead-end job. Every time something went wrong, he grasped for someone else to blame— a boss who didn't appreciate him, women who "didn't understand" his grind, friends who "betrayed" him by drifting away. He muttered, *"If only…"* so often it became his mantra. *"If only I had the right opportunities."*

"If only people weren't against me."

"If only life wasn't so damn hard."

But beneath all these complaints, a quiet dread gnawed at Dante's insides. He worked hard—he knew he wasn't lazy. He had decent ideas—he knew he wasn't stupid. Yet he remained stuck, running in circles, suspicious that the real problem lay somewhere closer than he dared to admit.

One cold evening after his shift, his old car rattled and died on a dark stretch of road. With numb fingers, he called a tow truck he couldn't afford. Sitting behind the wheel, fogging the windshield with his frustrated breaths, Dante slammed his fists on the dashboard. "Why does this keep happening to me?" he shouted into the empty night. His voice ricocheted back, offering no answers.

When he finally got home, he tossed his keys onto a cluttered coffee table and dropped onto the sagging couch. His apartment was a testament to neglect: laundry piled in corners, unopened bills scattered like fallen leaves, empty pizza boxes serving as monuments to evenings lost in bitterness.

He glanced at a small mirror on the wall. Its corner was cracked, distorting the image so he never had to see himself clearly. Normally, he avoided it, but tonight, his eyes lingered.

He turned away quickly, refusing to face what the reflection might say.

The Breaking Point

A few weeks later, Dante lost his job. Officially, it was due to "downsizing," but he knew his attitude and constant griping hadn't helped. He told himself the company was unfair, but a prickling shame nagged at him. He'd arrived late too many times and delivered mediocre work because he felt unappreciated. If he was honest, he hadn't given them a reason to value him.

That night, the apartment felt suffocating. The mirror seemed to call him, daring him to look. He tried to busy himself—flipping through TV channels, scrolling aimlessly on his phone—but the lure was too strong. Eventually, he stood before the cracked glass, unable to turn away this time.

His reflection stared back, hollow-eyed and worn. He saw a man weighed down by anger and resentment who had spent years crafting excuses instead of solutions. The truth pressed against his chest, making it hard to breathe.

The Voice of the Source

"Dante, stop lying to yourself. The problem isn't the world. The problem isn't them. The problem is you."

The words fell like thunder, rattling his heart. He wanted to deny it, to fling another excuse, but something about the voice's calm certainty broke through his defenses.

"You've spent your life pointing fingers, building walls, and hiding from the truth. But the mirror doesn't lie. It shows you exactly what you've become—not to punish you, but to wake you up. Everything you're running from is here, staring back at you."

Dante's knees felt weak. He gripped the edge of the dresser, knuckles whitening. The voice was unrelenting but not cruel; it spoke as if it cared about his freedom more than his comfort.

"The life you're living is the sum of your choices, habits, and mindset. The setbacks you blame on others? They began with you. But hear this: the same power that forged your chains can break them. The question is, will you own it?"

He shivered, tears gathering at the corners of his eyes. Owning his role in his downfall meant admitting he'd wasted years looking outward instead of inward.

"Radical accountability is not weakness. It is the path to freedom. Own your flaws, your mistakes, your choices, and you will own your power. Deny them, and you will remain trapped in the same cycle.
The mirror doesn't condemn you—it offers you the key. The choice is yours."

The Law of Radical Accountability

"You cannot change what you refuse to confront. The mirror shows you your truth so you can rewrite your story. Stop hiding from your reflection and start building your redemption."

Dante understood now: every time he blamed someone else, he chained himself tighter to his circumstances. If he wanted to break free, he had to face himself fully without flinching.

How to Break Free Through the Mirror

1. *Look Without Filters (Face the Truth)*

   "The mirror doesn't care about your ego. It only shows what is real. See it with courage." Dante realized the first step was seeing himself honestly.

   Action Step: Stand in front of a mirror. Ask yourself, "What truth am I avoiding about my life?" Write down every honest answer, no matter how painful.

2. *Stop Blaming Others (Take Back Your Power)*

   "Blame is the lie you tell yourself to stay comfortable. Stop giving others control over your life." Dante saw that blaming others gave them power over his fate. He needed to reclaim that power by acknowledging his role in every failure.

   Action Step: Identify one area of your life where you've been blaming others. Write down how your choices contributed to the situation.

3. *Forgive Yourself (Let Go of the Weight)*

"Accountability is not punishment. Forgiveness is the bridge to growth."

He realized that facing his truth wasn't about self-loathing— it was about release. He could forgive himself, learn from his mistakes, and move forward, lighter and freer.

Action Step: Write a letter to yourself, acknowledging your mistakes but also forgiving yourself for them. Commit to doing better.

4. *Change the Reflection (Act with Purpose)*

"The reflection doesn't change until you do. Move differently, and the image in the mirror will transform."

Realizing the truth meant little if he didn't act. He had to take tangible steps to align his life with the person he wanted to be.

Action Step: Choose one area of your life—work, relationships, or habits—and take one concrete action today to align it with the person you want to become.

Esoteric Insight: The Mirror is the Key

"The mirror doesn't lie, but it doesn't condemn either. It is the doorway to your liberation, the bridge to your highest self. Every flaw it reveals is an invitation to rise. Every truth it shows is a step toward freedom. The question is: will you walk through the door, or will you keep hiding from yourself?"

Dante now understood that the mirror was an ally, not an enemy. For years, he'd avoided confronting his own image —his own role in the life he'd built. Now, he stepped closer, tears drying on his cheeks, a quiet resolve forming in his chest.

The Final Word

The voice concluded:

"Dante, the mirror has always been waiting. It is not your enemy—it is your greatest ally. Stop fearing your reflection. Stop running from your truth. The power to break free is not in the world. It is here: in your hands, in your choices, in your reflection.

The mirror doesn't lie. It shows you what you are and who you can become. The question is: will you own the reflection and rise, or will you turn away and stay the same?"

Dante didn't turn away this time. He started small—tidying his apartment, making amends with an old friend he'd treated poorly, and applying for a new job with a mindset focused on solutions rather than blame. Over time, his reflection changed; no longer hollow-eyed and bitter, it became steady and determined.

Now it's your turn.

What are you running from? What truth is the mirror trying to show you? The time for denial is over.

The time for ownership has begun.

The question is: Will you face yourself or keep hiding in the shadows of blame?

CHAPTER 7

The Storm That Shapes Us

The Voice of Truth

Chaos isn't your curse—it's your calling.

The world tells you to fear the storm, cling to safety, and wait for calmer waters before you move. But hear this truth: nothing great is built in comfort. Chaos is not here to destroy you—it's here to awaken you.

Chaos is the fire that burns away what no longer serves you. It strips you down to your rawest self, forcing you to confront your fear, doubt, and limits. But if you embrace it, chaos becomes your ally. It becomes the currency that buys your transformation.

You can run from the storm, or you can become it. The choice is yours.

The Story: Jayden and the Firestorm Within

At nineteen, Jayden felt like he lived in a world forever buffering, as if his life's loading screen never reached 100%. He had dreams that pulsed under his skin—dreams of building a legendary gaming team that could rise through the ranks of the biggest tournaments, sign high-level sponsorships, and become a force in an arena where few dared to aim high. He craved the chance to prove himself, to turn latenight gaming sessions into a platform that showcased his skill and vision.

But all he had now was chaos.

His home felt like a pressure chamber on the verge of exploding. Working two jobs, his mother left the apartment before sunrise and stumbled back well past dusk, worn to the bone. Jayden watched the way she winced at the sight of unpaid bills, how her shoulders sagged under invisible weights. In her tired eyes, he saw love and fatigue entwined.

His stepdad, Tim, brought a different tension altogether —he saw Jayden's aspirations as childish distractions. *"Gaming won't pay the rent,"* he'd say, his tone dripping with disdain. Each dismissive comment hit Jayden like a taunt, daring him to prove otherwise.

Jayden's battles weren't only at home. Inside his own head, doubts whispered whenever he tried to strategize a move forward. How do you even start a professional team when you barely have money for decent gear, let alone tournament fees? Who would take him seriously, a kid with no contacts and unreliable internet? Would his potential wither under the weight of these questions?

And outside, life's chaos circled like a swarm. The internet at home lagged mercilessly, making every online match a gamble. His friends teased him—*"Lagging again?"*—but he heard the pity behind their jokes. Then, there was his part-time job at the gas station, barely covering his outdated gaming setup. Every extra dollar vanished into the family's black hole of expenses.

He felt trapped, each day a loop of frustration, ambition, and uncertainty.

The Day Everything Crashed

On a Friday night, Jayden tried to push forward. He planned a practice session with his online teammates, determined to test a new strategy he'd been thoroughly refining in his head all week. If it worked, it could become his team's signature play, a step toward standing out in a crowded field of competitors.

But chaos had other plans.

In the middle of the match, the internet cut out. From the other room, he heard Tim shouting, accusing Jayden of hogging bandwidth. His mom tried to calm things down, but the argument erupted into fullblown yelling. Suddenly, Tim slammed the router in a fit of rage, severing Jayden's connection —and the fragile peace he clung to. His match ended with a humiliating disconnect, and in that instant, everything he fought for seemed to crack like cheap glass.

Jayden retreated to his room, fury and shame twisting in his chest. Messages from his teammates flashed on his screen:

"What happened?"

"You good, bro?"

But Jayden couldn't answer. He stared at his reflection in the black screen—a boy trapped between a dream and a storm, a restless spirit weighed down by everyday chaos. He wanted to scream at the unfairness, to punch through the walls, boxing him in, or to just walk away from it all. Instead, he slumped onto his bed, staring at the peeling paint on the ceiling.

"Why is it always like this?" he whispered. There was no one to answer. The hum of his idle computer and the muffled voices outside were his only company.

Time stretched. The tension in the air felt different this time as if something beneath the surface of his frustration was shifting. Not a sound, not a flash of light, but a presence—an undeniable force rising within him. A whisper of something bigger than his doubts, stronger than his rage.

Then, like thunder rolling through a distant canyon, the voice came.

The Voice of the Source

"Jayden, why do you fear the storm when you were made to rise in it?"

The words electrified him. His heart pounded, but he didn't feel fear—he felt recognition.

"You think chaos is your enemy, but it's the fire that forges you. Every great story begins in the storm. Every legend is built in the rubble of destruction. The world isn't falling apart around you—it's breaking apart to show you what's possible."

He felt tears burning at the corners of his eyes, not of sadness, but of understanding. He had expected life to wait for him, to roll out a red carpet of perfect conditions. But the voice told him otherwise:
"You've been waiting for the perfect moment, the perfect plan, the perfect conditions. But perfection is a lie. Growth doesn't come from calm. It comes from chaos—the moments when everything feels like it's burning, and you choose to rise anyway."

The voice swelled, flooding the room with its certainty:

"The chaos in your life is not here to destroy you—it's here to awaken you. The doubt you feel, the fights at home, the broken plans—they are not roadblocks. They are the currency you must pay to become who you are meant to be. The storm is not your enemy—it's your proving ground."

The Law of Chaos

"Chaos is the fire that burns away weakness, the storm that reveals your strength. Embrace it, and you will rise. Fear it, and you will stay small. The choice is yours."

Jayden realized that chaos wasn't a sign of failure; it was the crucible of his transformation. He'd been trying to avoid it, waiting for calm waters, but now he understood that storms forge warriors, not victims.

How to Turn Chaos into Growth

1. *Reframe the Storm (Chaos is Your Teacher)*

   "Chaos isn't here to punish you—it's here to prepare you."

   Jayden saw that every setback, every argument, every lagging connection was teaching him resilience, patience, and adaptability.

   Action Step: Identify one area of your life that feels chaotic. Write down what this chaos is teaching you—about patience, resilience, or creativity.

2. *Take One Step (Move Through the Storm)*

   "The storm doesn't end by waiting. It ends when you move."

   He realized he didn't need ideal conditions to start forming his team. He could begin with what he had, even if it was imperfect.

   Action Step: Choose one small action you can take toward your goal today, even if the situation isn't ideal.

3. **Turn Pain Into Power (Transmute the Energy)**

"Every setback carries the seed of strength. Use it to build."

The rage and frustration he felt could be channeled into focus, pushing him to work harder, smarter, and with more determination.

Action Step: When you feel overwhelmed by chaos, write down three ways you can use that energy to push forward.

4. **Build in the Fire (Create While You Struggle)**

"The best creations are born in the storm, not after it."

Jayden decided to start recruiting teammates—people who shared his vision—despite the slow internet, the tension at home, and his tight budget.

Action Step: Start building your vision today, even if the timing feels wrong. Chaos is not the enemy of creation—it's its birthplace.

Esoteric Insight: Chaos is the Currency of Transformation

"The storm you fear is the fire you need. It will strip away your excuses, shatter your limits, and force you to rise. Chaos is not destruction—it's the currency you must pay to become unstoppable."

Jayden finally understood that chaos was not just random suffering— it was his initiation, his path to becoming the person he needed to be.

The Final Word

The voice concluded:

"Jayden, the chaos in your life is not here to break you—it's here to shape you. The fire burns, but it also forges. The storm rages, but it also clears the path.

The question is not whether chaos will come—it already has. The question is: will you let it consume you, or will you use it to rise? The storm is your proving ground. Step into it, and become the legend you were born to be."

Jayden wiped his eyes, his heart steady for the first time in months. He resolved to stop waiting for perfect conditions and build his gaming team with the tools he had, forging alliances and strategies even in the midst of chaos. Over time, the turbulence no longer felt like a curse—it became the force driving his evolution.

Now it's your turn.

What chaos are you facing? What storm is calling you to rise? The time for fear is over. The time for transformation has begun.

The question is: *Will you embrace the storm, or will you run from it?*

CHAPTER 8

The Illusion of Time Master the Clock, Command Your Destiny

The Voice of Truth

Time is not your ally.

The world will tell you that you have time—time to wait, time to procrastinate, time to waste on things that don't matter. It's a lie. Time is the one resource you can never get back. Every second wasted is a debt your future self will pay.

But hear this truth: time isn't your enemy—it's your tool.

The problem isn't time itself; it's your illusion of it. You think you have more than you do. You think tomorrow will always come. But time waits for no one. The question is: will you master it or let it master you?

The Story: Elijah and Aaron, Two Paths Diverged

Elijah and Aaron grew up like brothers, sharing a world defined by scarcity and survival. They knew each other's families, played ball on cracked asphalt, and dreamed under the same flickering streetlights. In the quiet hours after the neighborhood fell asleep, they'd whisper about the futures they wanted—futures that didn't end in dead-end jobs or empty wallets.

Both carried big dreams. Elijah's was to start a media company that would amplify voices like theirs— unseen, unheard, often dismissed. He envisioned documentaries that shed light on hidden struggles, podcasts sparking meaningful conversations, and short films that inspire change.

Aaron's dream took a different shape but carried the same longing. He wanted to build a clothing line that told their story in fabric and thread, a brand that would pay homage to their block and their shared struggle.

At twenty-two, they stood side by side at the threshold of adulthood, each holding their vision like a precious gem. They promised each other they'd make it out and come back for the rest.

But that's where their paths began to diverge.

Elijah: The Disciplined Visionary

Elijah understood something most people ignored: time would not slow down for him. He had watched too many neighbors and cousins grow old, waiting for "the right time" to chase their dreams.

He refused to be another story of untapped potential.

Every moment mattered to him. He rose before dawn, mapping out his day. Mornings became sacred hours of planning and execution— sending emails, scripting podcast episodes, reaching out to local artists, and editing rough footage. In the afternoons, he sought knowledge, reading books, watching tutorials, and building relationships with mentors. Evenings were reserved for reflection and recalibration. He treated time like borrowed money—any second spent idly had to be justified.

It wasn't easy. Friends teased him for turning down parties and for not binge-watching the latest series. But Elijah's silence in the face of their invitations wasn't arrogance—it was reverence for the seconds slipping through the hourglass. He knew every distraction stole energy from his dream.

Slowly, the pieces came together. Elijah launched a podcast that resonated with an audience hungry for authentic voices. He collaborated with local creatives to produce short films that garnered attention. Small wins started to accumulate like droplets in a bucket until he realized he was no longer just dreaming—he was building a legacy.

Aaron: The Dreamer Lost in the Illusion

Aaron shared Elijah's hunger, but he viewed time differently. He believed he had plenty of it. Waking up late, he'd scroll through social media, reassuring himself that he'd work on his clothing brand "later." He sketched a few designs, shared them with friends who nodded approvingly, but he never took that next big step. When the weekends came, Aaron said yes to every invitation, telling himself he was living life, enjoying his youth. He convinced himself he was making progress simply because he talked about his dream so often.

But talking and doing were worlds apart.

Days turned into months, and months into years. He began to notice Elijah shining, while he remained stuck at the start line. Aaron told himself he was waiting—for the perfect moment, the perfect opportunity, the perfect sign. He believed time would eventually deliver that break; he just had to be patient.

Then, one day, as he scrolled through his phone one day at twentyfive, he realized Elijah's company was thriving: a small team of passionate people, projects in motion, new opportunities knocking. Meanwhile, Aaron's designs were still just sketches in an old notebook, his ideas trapped in a future that never arrived.

The Breaking Point

One afternoon, Aaron decided to visit Elijah's office. He hadn't seen his old friend in months —perhaps because it hurt to see someone who'd taken the steps he himself refused to take.

As he stepped inside, Aaron felt an electric energy in the air. Cameras, laptops, and a quiet hum of purpose filled the room. He saw Elijah reviewing footage with a collaborator, deep in discussion. When Elijah noticed Aaron, he smiled—warm, genuine, and confident, like a man who had earned his place in the world.

"I'm proud of you, man," Aaron said, struggling to keep the tremor out of his voice. He couldn't ignore the pang of regret twisting in his gut.

Elijah nodded. "Thanks, bro. But what about you? How's the clothing line?"

Aaron hesitated, shame creeping up his spine. He had no progress to show, just excuses he'd recycled too many times. "I haven't started yet. I've been...busy," he lied, knowing they both recognized it.

Elijah didn't condemn him, but his words were clear as cut glass: "Time doesn't wait, Aaron. If you don't move now, it'll move without you."

Aaron left, haunted by that truth. He knew Elijah was right. Time had not waited for him, and now it felt like it was slipping through his fingers like sand he couldn't grasp.

The Voice of the Source

That night, Aaron sat alone in his room, silent, his dreams weighing heavier than ever before. For the first time, he realized that the hours and days he'd treated so casually were precious currency he'd squandered.

Then the voice came, steady and undeniable:

"Aaron, do you feel it? The seconds slipping through your fingers? The dreams you're burying with every delay? Time isn't your enemy, but it isn't your friend either. It is the one thing you cannot control, but it is the one thing you must master."

Aaron's eyes stung with unshed tears. He saw his future self, older and still waiting —and it terrified him.

"You think you have time, but that is the greatest illusion of all. Tomorrow is not promised. Every second you waste is stolen from the man you are meant to become. The question is: will you spend your time building your dream, or will you let it slip away?"

The voice sharpened, cutting through his denial:

"Elijah understood this truth: the clock is always ticking. He moved with urgency, not because he was afraid, but because he respected the gift of time. You, Aaron, have been treating it like an endless river, but it is a drying well. Decide now—will you honor your time, or will you squander it?"

The Law of Time

"Time waits for no one. Master it, and you master your life. Waste it, and it will bury your dreams."

Aaron realized he had been his own obstacle, pretending he had forever. He vowed not to let another day drift by without action.

How to Command Time and Build Your Destiny

1. Respect the Clock (Stop Delaying)

"The clock doesn't care about your excuses. Move with urgency."

Aaron understood that every casual shrug, every "later," stole from his potential.

Action Step: Write down three things you've been putting off. Commit to starting one of them today, no matter how small.

2. Eliminate Distractions (Protect Your Focus)

"The enemy of time is distraction. Guard your time like your life depends on it—because it does."

Elijah thrived because he cut distractions from his goals before they cut him off. Aaron saw the difference.

Action Step: Identify your top three distractions—social media, TV, unproductive habits—and set boundaries to limit their impact.

3. Prioritize the Dream (Make Every Hour Count)

"Time is not infinite. Prioritize what matters, or you'll spend your life chasing what doesn't." Aaron realized he had to invest his best hours in his dream, not just his leftover time.

Action Step: Plan your day with intention. Block out time for your most important goals, and stick to it like your future depends on it.

4. *Move With Urgency (Act Like Time is Running Out)*

"The clock is always ticking. Act now, or regret later."

Elijah's secret wasn't luck; it was urgency. Aaron resolved to act before conditions felt perfect. **Action Step:** Take one bold action toward your dream today. Don't wait for the perfect moment —it doesn't exist.

Esoteric Insight: The Illusion of Time

"Time is the most precious currency you have. Every second is a seed—plant it wisely, or watch it wither. The illusion of time is thinking you have more of it. The truth of time is knowing it waits for no one."

Aaron understood now that time was neither enemy nor friend; it was a resource he had to spend wisely before it disappeared.

The Final Word

The voice concluded:

*"Aaron, the clock is ticking. Your excuses are not valid, and your delays are not justified. Time is slipping through your fingers, but it's not too late—if you act now.

The question is not whether time will pass—it will. The question is: will you pass with it, or will you rise before it runs out? Your future is waiting, but the clock won't stop.

The pieces are in your hands. Move now, or stay behind."*

Aaron took the lesson to heart. He stopped the endless scrolling, scheduled time for design work, and reached out to a mentor who could guide him. Slowly, he began to move with the urgency Elijah had always embodied. Every hour he reclaimed brought him closer to making his vision real.

Now it's your turn.

What have you been putting off? What excuses have you been making? Time waits for no one.

The question is: *Will you rise, or will you let the clock run out?*

CHAPTER 9

The Law of Seasons Honor the Cycle, Respect the Harvest

The Voice of Truth

The world moves in seasons.

Nature knows this. The trees do not bear fruit in winter, the flowers do not bloom before the frost melts, and the farmer does not harvest before the seeds have taken root. But you? You rush what cannot be rushed.

Hear this truth: every season has a purpose.

The winter of your life is not here to punish you but to prepare you. The spring is not here to overwhelm you—it is here to grow you. And the harvest will not come until the work has been done.

Rush the season, and you will ruin the harvest. Respect the cycle, and the fruits of your labor will thrive.

The Story: Mia and the Rushed Harvest

Mia had never been one to wait. Growing up, she watched her grandmother slowly, patiently knead dough or steep herbs, insisting that every good thing took its proper time. Young and restless, Mia struggled to understand why her grandmother never hurried. In Mia's world, everything felt like a race —rushing to school to get a better job and prove herself.

By twenty-six, Mia had made impatience her trademark. She avoided long lines, cursed slow traffic, and bristled at the slightest delay. If life was a journey, Mia wanted to sprint straight to the finish line.

But now she carried a dream so tender and beautiful that it demanded what she'd always resisted: **Patience.**

She wanted to build a wellness brand—natural skincare products infused with love and tradition. Inspired by her late grandmother's kitchen remedies, Mia envisioned creams and oils that nourished not just the skin but the soul. Yet despite her noble intentions, her impatience threatened to rip the dream from its roots before it could bloom.

The Beginning of the Dream

Mia quit her stable retail job without a second thought. "It's now or never," she told herself. She had some savings, a handful of notes from her grandmother's old recipes, and the fierce conviction that success favored the bold. She watched tutorials, sketched product labels, and sourced ingredients online. By the end of one hectic month, she thought she was ready to launch.

Friends and family cheered her on at a small launch party where her first batch of creams and body oils sold modestly. The initial positive feedback buoyed her spirits. She imagined her brand's name on storefronts, her products flying off shelves. She assured herself that it was only a matter of time before her vision fully materialized.

But Mia had skipped steps. She had never tested the consistency of her creams through a full product cycle. She had never given her formulas time to settle, adjust, and improve. She had sown seeds and immediately demanded a harvest.

The Struggles Begin

Problems surfaced like weeds in a rushed garden. By the third batch, customers were complaining about separated creams and leaking oils. Mia brushed off the warnings, convinced it was just a minor hiccup. Instead of pausing to refine her process, she charged ahead, patching leaks with band-aid solutions.

Financial pressure mounted. Ingredients cost more than she'd estimated, and packaging and shipping fees quickly added up. Her savings drained faster than she had anticipated, and modest sales couldn't keep pace with mounting expenses. Panic gnawed at her stomach. Desperate, she borrowed money from a friend and invested in online ads, hoping quick exposure would solve her problems.

But ads brought attention, not trust, and without trust, sales stalled.

Soon, she was drowning in unsold inventory and overdue bills. The stress weighed on her chest like a stone. She found herself questioning why her dream —so pure and meaningful —was slipping through her fingers.

The Breaking Point

Late one night, under the dim light of her apartment's lone lamp, Mia found herself surrounded by unopened packages and a phone buzzing with refund requests. Tears blurred her vision. She dropped onto her knees, sobbing quietly, shame and regret flooding her heart.

"Why is this happening to me?" she whispered, looking at the faded photograph of her grandmother on the wall. That gentle smile once gave Mia reassurance. Now, it felt like a distant memory.

"I'm trying, Grandma," she said softly Her voice breaking. "I'm trying so hard. Why isn't it enough?"

The silence in the room felt heavy, but then it stretched out. Something shifted. It felt as if the air thickened with presence. A voice emerged—not scolding, not angry, but firm and steady.

The Voice of the Source

"Mia, why are you rushing the season? Why do you demand the fruits of harvest when you have not prepared the soil, nurtured the roots, or let the rain do its work?"

Mia held her breath, tears drying on her cheeks.

"You are trying to force what cannot be forced. Success is not a sprint—it is a cycle. Winter teaches patience. Spring brings growth. Summer demands nurture. And only then does autumn give its reward. But you, Mia, have tried to skip the seasons. And now, you wonder why the fruit is bitter."

The words pierced her heart. For the first time, she saw her impatience clearly, how she had plucked the fruit before it was ripe and now tasted only bitterness.

"Every season has its purpose. The winter of your struggle is here to teach you strength. The spring of your effort is here to demand your focus. The summer of your preparation is here to refine you. But the harvest will not come until you honor these seasons. Rush the process, and you will ruin the result." The voice softened, but its message remained unyielding:

"You are not failing, Mia. You are growing. But growth demands patience. It demands surrender to the rhythm of life. The soil of your dream is rich, but only if you trust the process. Stop rushing, and let the harvest come in its time."

The Law of Seasons "Every dream moves through seasons. Winter teaches patience. Spring demands effort. Summer requires care. And only in autumn can you harvest. Honor your season, and the cycle will honor you."

Mia realized she had acted like a farmer who plants seeds and demands fruit the very next morning. She understood now that each stage had a purpose, and ignoring it meant sabotaging her own success.

How to Align With the Law of Seasons

1. Recognize Your Season (Know Where You Are)

"You cannot thrive until you understand where you are in the cycle."

Mia realized her frustration stemmed from expecting harvesttime results in a planting season. She learned that clarity about her current stage was the first step towards aligning with the process.

Action Step: Reflect on your journey. Are you in winter (planning), spring (building), summer (nurturing), or autumn (harvesting)? Please write it down, acknowledge it, and accept it.

2. **Focus on the Work (Respect the Process)**

   "The farmer doesn't demand fruit before the tree has grown. Do the work that matches your season."

   Mia realized she needed to refine her products and strengthen her business foundation before pushing for more sales.

   Respecting the process meant slowing down to build something lasting.

   Action Step: Identify one action that aligns with your current season. Commit to it fully instead of rushing ahead.

3. **Practice Patience (Trust the Timing)**

   "Impatience destroys what patience builds. Growth happens in its own time, not yours." She learned that patience wasn't passive but an active choice to trust the process and continue working with faith.

   Action Step: Create a timeline that reflects your goals' natural growth. Focus on making consistent progress, not instant results.

4. **Prepare for the Harvest (Be Ready to Receive)**

   "The harvest doesn't come to those who wait—it comes to those who prepare."

   Mia began organizing her finances, researching better suppliers, and establishing systems to handle future orders so that when success arrived, she could properly welcome it.

   Action Step: Write down three ways you can prepare for success, even if it feels far away.

Esoteric Insight: The Rhythm of Life

"Life is not a straight line—it is a cycle, a rhythm, a dance between effort and surrender. Every season is necessary. Winter shapes you. Spring stretches you. Summer strengthens you. And autumn rewards you. Rush the cycle, and you will ruin the harvest. Honor the rhythm, and life will align in your favor." Mia finally understood that her journey was like her grandmother's recipes—nothing could be rushed without spoiling the outcome. Each step, each season, had its purpose.

The Final Word

The voice concluded:

"Mia, the dream you carry is not dying—it is growing. But you must honor its seasons. Stop rushing.

Stop doubting. Trust the rhythm, and the harvest will come.

The question is not whether success will come. It will. The question is: will you have the patience to see it through? The soil has been planted. The work is underway.

Will you honor the season, or will you destroy the harvest before it's ready?"

Mia took the lesson to heart. She slowed down, refocused on building a solid foundation, and stopped demanding immediate results. Over time, her brand began to grow steadily and sustainably, reflecting the care and wisdom she poured into it.

Now It's Your Turn.

What season are you in? Are you planting, nurturing, or harvesting? The time for impatience is over.

The time for honoring your season has begun.

***The question is:** Will you align with the rhythm, or will you rush and ruin the harvest?*

CHAPTER 10

The Masks We Wear Drop the Disguise, Reclaim Your Power

The Voice of Truth

You wear a mask.

You tell yourself it's for protection—that the world is too cruel, too judgmental to see the real you. So you cover yourself, layer by layer until the person staring back at you in the mirror is a stranger.

You wear the mask to fit in, to survive, to avoid judgment. But hear this truth: the mask is not your salvation but your prison.

The mask hides you from your pain, but it also hides you from your destiny. It protects you from rejection, but it also blocks your blessings.

The time has come to drop the disguise. To stop pretending. To stop hiding. The world doesn't need the version of you the mask creates. It needs the real you—the raw, unfiltered, undeniable truth of who you are.

The question is: will you choose authenticity or will you let the mask suffocate your power?

The Story: Four Masks, Four Traps

Four people sat in the same café, each wearing a mask and holding their breath behind it. They didn't know each other's names, but they shared the same secret—the fear that their true selves weren't enough.

1. Aaliyah: The Perfectionist

> Aaliyah entered the café with perfect makeup, immaculate hair, and heels that clicked confidently. At a glance, she looked untouchable: a high-ranking corporate executive who had everything under control. She had fought hard for her place in that office tower, outsmarting obstacles others never knew existed. But the cost was high.

Each day demanded more of her—longer hours, higher stakes, more challenging deadlines. Behind the polished exterior, she was unraveling. Sleep eluded her. Anxiety gnawed at her. She despised the work that had once inspired her. But she couldn't let anyone see her struggles. **Perfection was her armor.**

The mask of perfection pressed down on her chest. She smiled when she wanted to cry and said, "I'm fine," when she was drowning. She believed the mask made her strong, but in truth, it was suffocating her.

2. Marcus: The Chameleon

> In a corner booth, Marcus laughed at jokes that didn't amuse him and agreed with opinions he found empty. He was here with

colleagues who all seemed to belong to a world of designer suits and golf weekends. Marcus, however, felt like an imposter among them, unsure he deserved a seat at this table.

He'd learned long ago that blending in prevented rejection. At school, at work, and at parties, he changed colors like a chameleon, mirroring those around him. It kept him safe, he told himself. But deep down, he knew the truth: he never voiced his honest thoughts or shared his perspective. He sacrificed **authenticity for acceptance.**

The mask he wore promised him safety but delivered loneliness. He wanted to roar like a lion, to stand firm in his truth, yet he kept acting like a sheep to avoid being cast out.

3. Jamal: The Hustler

Leaning against the counter, Jamal scrolled through his phone, projecting a swagger he didn't truly feel. He wore the mask of the "hustler"—a man who had it all figured out, who needed no one's help. Growing up in a rough neighborhood, he'd learned that vulnerability meant weakness. He swore he'd never beg, never show need.

Behind his mask, he struggled to keep the lights on. The grind he boasted about barely paid the bills. Still, he wouldn't dare ask for assistance. To him, pride was survival. Yet this pride was strangling his potential. Without asking for guidance or support, he remained stuck, arms folded, back against a wall he'd built himself.

The mask told him, **"Real men don't ask for help."** But the truth was that his strength lay beneath that lie, waiting to be freed.

4. Sofia: The Invisible One

By the window, Sofia cradled her cup of tea, head bowed low. She slipped into rooms unnoticed, never speaking too loudly, never doing anything that might draw a second glance. The world had taught her that standing out attracted ridicule, so she made herself small.

She avoided compliments, avoided confrontation, avoided the risk of being seen and judged.

But invisibility came at a cost. Sofia wasn't living—she was hiding. She longed to share her ideas, her art, her gentle kindness. Yet she believed blending into the background was the only way to avoid pain.

Her mask promised safety in the shadows, but it robbed her of light.

The Catalyst

The café buzzed softly with the hum of conversation and the clink of spoons against ceramic cups. Then, as if the air itself shifted, a man stood up—a stranger with an aura of calm intensity. He didn't raise his voice, but his words commanded the room.

"I can see your masks," he said, his tone neither cruel nor mocking but filled with compassion and clarity.

Aaliyah's heart skipped a beat. Marcus stopped laughing. Jamal lowered his phone. Sofia lifted her eyes.

The Voice of the Source

"You wear the mask to survive, but it is killing you. You wear the mask to protect yourself, but it is robbing you of everything you are meant to be."

He looked at each of them in turn, his gaze steady, his words cutting straight to their core.

"Aaliyah, your perfection is a lie. You think the mask makes you strong, but it is the reason you are breaking. Your power is in your truth, not your façade."

Aaliyah felt tears prick in her eyes. She yearned to be real, show her exhaustion, and admit she needed help. The voice gave her permission.

"Marcus, you are not a chameleon. You are a lion pretending to be a sheep. You think blending in will keep you safe, but it is why you feel invisible."

Marcus's throat tightened. He realized he had given up his voice for the illusion of acceptance. What if his true voice was what the world needed all along?

"Jamal, your pride is a chain. You think asking for help makes you weak, but it is your refusal to ask that keeps you small. Your strength is in vulnerability."

Jamal's chest ached. Could it be that letting down his guard would set him free?

"Sofia, your invisibility is not protection—it is imprisonment. You were not born to hide. You were born to shine."

Sofia's heart fluttered. She imagined speaking up, being seen, and feeling the sunlight on her face instead of hiding in shadows.

"The mask protects you, but it also hides you. It blocks your pain, but it also blocks your power. If you want to live —truly live — you must drop the disguise. The world doesn't need your mask— it needs your truth. Your real power comes when you show your real self."

The Law of Authenticity "Your mask is your prison. Drop it, and you will rise. Show your truth, and the world will align in your favor."

They realized the mask wasn't keeping them safe—it was keeping them small. The world needed their authentic gifts, not the watereddown versions they offered.

How to Drop the Mask and Reclaim Your Power

1. *Identify Your Mask (Name the Lie)*

"You cannot break free until you admit what you are hiding behind."

They began to recognize their masks for what they were—
Aaliyah's perfectionism, Marcus's chameleon act, Jamal's pride, and Sofia's invisibility. The first step was acknowledging the lie they were living.

Action Step: Reflect on your life. What mask are you wearing to fit in, avoid judgment, or feel safe? Write it down.

2. *Confront the Fear (Face the Truth)*

"The mask is built on fear. Confront the fear, and the mask will fall."

They understood the root of their disguises—fear of being found lacking, rejection, and vulnerability. The fear had dictated their choices, but now they could name it.

Action Step: Ask yourself, "What am I afraid will happen if I show my true self?" Write down the answer.

3. *Take a Small Step (Test the Waters)*

   "You don't have to rip off the mask in one day. Start small, and let your truth grow." Aaliyah decided to admit she was overwhelmed by a trusted friend. Marcus dared to voice an opinion that was truly his. Jamal reached out for advice for the first time. Sofia raised her voice enough to be heard.

   Action Step: Choose one area of your life where you can show your authentic self today. Take one small step.

4. *Build a New Habit (Live Unmasked)*

   "The mask will try to creep back. Stay vigilant, and choose authenticity daily."

   They knew the journey wouldn't be over in a single day. The mask would try to return, whispering old fears. But they committed to practicing authenticity until it became as natural as breathing. They had to practice choosing truth over pretense.

   Action Step: Create a daily affirmation: **"I am enough as I am. My truth is my power."** Repeat it every morning.

Esoteric Insight: The Mask is the Barrier

"The mask hides you from judgment, but it also hides you from love. It protects you from rejection, but it also blocks your destiny. The time for hiding is over. The time for truth has come. Drop the mask, and the world will see the power you've been hiding."

They came to understand a profound truth: the mask had stolen from them the very things they craved—belonging, success, growth. Only their authentic selves could unlock their true potential.

The Final Word

The voice concluded:

"Aaliyah, Marcus, Jamal, Sofia—you are not your mask. The real you is stronger than the lies you wear. The question is not whether you can drop the mask—you can. The question is: will you?

The world is waiting for your truth. Will you show it, or will you let the mask suffocate your destiny?"

One by one, they made their choice:

- Aaliyah confessed her struggles and asked for support.
- Marcus dared to stand apart and speak honestly.
- Jamal opened up and found guidance that changed his path.
- Sofia stepped into the light, no longer content to be invisible.

Now It's Your Turn.

What mask are you wearing? What truth are you hiding? The time for disguises is over. The time for authenticity has begun.

The question is: *Will you drop the mask, or will you let it define you?*

CHAPTER 11

The Ladder and the Bridge Break Free, Build Your Ascent

The Voice of Truth

The ladder is a trap.

The world told you to climb. It gave you a ladder with endless rungs, each step promising success, validation, and belonging. But what they didn't tell you is this: the ladder isn't meant to take you to the top. It's meant to keep you climbing.

The higher you go, the farther you feel from where you're supposed to be. The ladder wasn't built for you—it was built to control, exhaust, and make you forget that you were never meant to climb someone else's path.

You were meant to build your own bridge.

A ladder locks you into their system, but a bridge takes you where you choose to go. A bridge isn't bound by their expectations—it's built by your vision, your effort, and your direction.

> *The question is: will you keep climbing the ladder, or will you stop, step back, and start building your bridge?*

The Story: Jacob and Selina, Two Ascent Paths

Jacob and Selina met as college freshmen, two dreamers who pulled all-nighters in the library, not just for exams but for the sheer thrill of planning futures bigger than themselves. They once believed they'd forge their own paths—together, side by side, building something that mattered.

But five years out of college, their lives looked nothing alike.

1. Jacob: The Ladder Climber

> Jacob grew up believing that stability and success came from following the rules: get a good job, climb the ranks, and earn respect. At first, this made sense. He took the corporate position everyone said was a "good start" and excelled because he worked hard and followed instructions. Each promotion felt like a small victory. Each raise whispered, "You're doing it right."

But as the years passed, something gnawed at him. The work felt hollow. He sat in meeting after meeting, his mind drifting toward unfulfilled passions he had never nurtured. He navigated office politics he despised and took on responsibilities he didn't care about. Yet he kept climbing because what else was he supposed to do?

By his fifth year, he was offered another promotion—better pay, a more impressive title. Instead of joy, he felt dread. That night, in his cramped bathroom, he stared at his reflection.

"Is this it?" he asked the mirror.

He remembered the younger version of himself, full of ideas and dreams, and wondered where that boy had gone. The weight in his chest answered for him: the ladder had weighed him down, rung by rung until he hardly recognized himself.

2. Selina: The Bridge Builder

> Selina started on a similar path: an entry-level job in marketing, a steady paycheck, and a future paved by someone else's roadmap. But two years in, she felt her soul grow restless. She had always loved storytelling—writing as a child under dim lamp light, crafting worlds that danced in her imagination. The job paid the bills, but it starved her spirit.

One day, her reflection confronted her, just as it did Jacob. She realized that if she stayed, she'd be climbing a ladder that didn't lead to the creative, fulfilling life she wanted. Against her family's advice and her friends' puzzled looks, she quit. She decided to build her own bridge—freelancing, writing, creating on her own terms.

It wasn't easy. The first year tested her resolve. Clients were scarce, rejection letters piled up, and her savings dwindled. Late at night, doubt whispered that she'd made a mistake. But she pressed on, planting planks under her feet one at a time. By the third year, she had published her first novel. It didn't make her wealthy, but it made her proud. She learned that each board she placed was a step toward freedom and authenticity.

The Breaking Point

Years passed with little contact between them, but one autumn afternoon, Jacob and Selina finally met for coffee in a quiet café downtown. The air smelled of cinnamon and hope.

Jacob studied her face. She looked tired but radiant as if every hardship had carved purpose into her features. "You're glowing," he said, almost envious.

Selina shrugged and laughed softly. "I'm tired, yes, and broke half the time. I'm figuring it out day by day. But I'm free." Her eyes sparkled with a quiet pride. "I'm happy, Jacob."

Jacob's shoulders sagged. He confessed that he felt stuck, climbing a ladder that led nowhere he wanted to go. Selina's heart ached for him. She reached across the table and took his hand. "Then stop climbing," she said gently. "You don't have to keep going up. Step back and build your bridge. It's harder, but it's yours."

Jacob's throat tightened. "What if I fall?"

Selina's smile was kind. "You might. But at least if you fall, you'll fall toward your own path, not someone else's."

The Voice of the Source

That night, Jacob sat alone in his silent apartment. The city lights outside blurred into abstract shapes on the window. He thought about Selina's words and the dreamer he once was before the ladder stole his courage.

Then, the voice emerged—not loud, but commanding:

"Jacob, you've been climbing their ladder for so long you've forgotten your own power. You traded your vision for their validation, your freedom for their structure. But hear me now: the ladder is not your path. The ladder is your cage."

He closed his eyes, tears slipping free.

"You think the ladder will take you to the top, but it won't. It keeps you climbing aimlessly until you forget why you started. The ladder is a lie. The bridge is your truth."

The voice struck him with painful clarity.

"The bridge is harder to build. It demands your strength, your vision, and your labor. But it leads to freedom, to a destiny you shape, not one they dictate. Will you keep climbing their ladder, or will you stop and start building your bridge?"

The Law of Ascent

"A ladder locks you into their path. A bridge takes you where you want to go. Stop climbing to fit in.

Start building to break out."

Jacob realized he had surrendered his dreams, piece by piece, to the comfort of a preset path. He saw now that comfort was a trap, and the cost was too high.

How to Build Your Bridge and Forge Your Own Path

1. *Recognize the Ladder (See the Trap)*

    "The ladder is not leading you to your dream—it's leading you into their system." Jacob understood he had chased promotions that served someone else's goals, not his own passion.

    Action Step: Reflect on your current path. Are you climbing toward your dream, or are you following someone else's map?

2. *Define Your Bridge (Clarify Your Destination)*

"The bridge doesn't build itself. You must know where it's meant to take you."

Selina's success came from aligning her actions with her true love—storytelling.

Action Step: Write down what you truly want—not what the world says you should want, but what sets your soul on fire.

3. *Step Back (Let Go of the Ladder)*

"You cannot build the bridge while climbing the ladder. Let go."

To begin, Jacob needed to release the rung he clung to, even if it meant fear and uncertainty.

Action Step: Identify one step you can take today to stop climbing someone else's ladder— whether quitting, pivoting, or starting a side hustle.

4. *Build Daily (Lay the Planks)*

"The bridge is built one plank at a time. Move with consistency."

Selina's bridge came from daily effort—writing pages, reaching out to clients, and honing her craft. **Action Step:** Commit to one habit that aligns with your dream. Build consistently, even when progress is slow.

Esoteric Insight: The Ladder vs. The Bridge

"The ladder traps you in their system. The bridge frees you to create your own. The ladder makes you climb aimlessly. The bridge gives you direction. The ladder was not built for you. The bridge is built by you. The time for climbing is over. The time for building has begun."

Jacob saw the truth now: the ladder never belonged to him. It was someone else's construct. His bridge would be his masterpiece.

The Final Word

The voice concluded:

*"Jacob, the ladder is not your destiny. It is their design. You were not born to climb endlessly. You were born to build deliberately.

The question is not whether you can climb the ladder—you can. The question is: will you stop long enough to build the bridge?

The ladder is their illusion. The bridge is your truth. Will you keep climbing their path, or will you construct your own?"*

Jacob dried his tears. He would stop. He would step back. He would dare to build something that reflected who he truly was. The progress wouldn't be quick or easy, but every plank he laid would bring him closer to the life he longed for.

Now it's your turn.

What ladder are you climbing? What bridge are you ignoring? The time for aimless climbing is over.

The time for purposeful building has begun.

The question is: Will you keep climbing their ladder, or will you build your bridge?

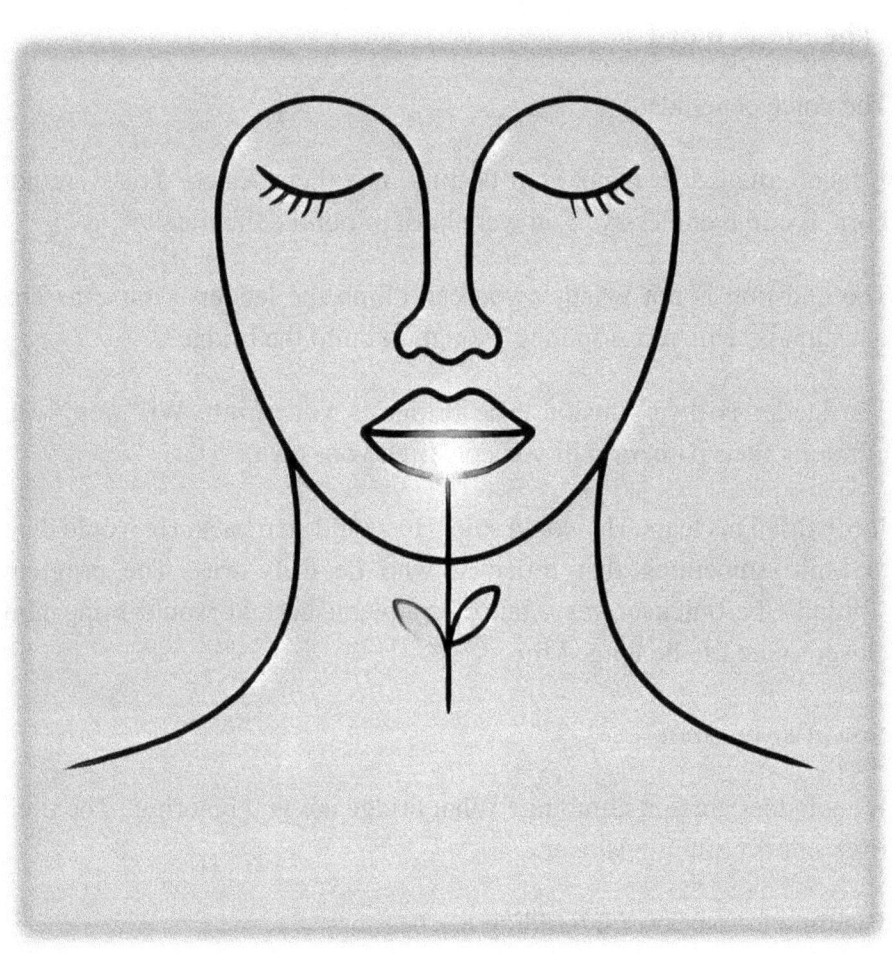

CHAPTER 12

The Power of Silence Speak Less, Move More

The Voice of Truth

The world taught you to talk—to explain, to justify, to beg for validation. It told you that your words are the currency of your worth and that you must constantly announce your intentions, share your plans, and seek approval.

But hear this truth: silence is power.

A quiet mind is a fortress no enemy can breach. A quiet move is a checkmate before the game even begins. The noise you create to be seen and heard is the same noise that weakens you, drains you, and exposes you.

The time for talking is over. The time for silence has come. Stop announcing your every move. Stop seeking their validation. Stop explaining yourself to those who will never understand. Move in silence, and let your results speak for you.

The Story: Nadia and Leon, The Battle of Noise and Quiet

Nadia and Leon grew up in the same tight-knit neighborhood, where the streets were lined with homes creaking under the weight of old dreams. It was a place where people talked big but often settled for less. Both vowed to break free, determined to carve lives beyond the limits they had inherited.

They shared the same hunger, the same spark, but chose different weapons. For Nadia, it was her voice. For Leon, it was his silence.

1. Nadia: The Loud Dreamer

Even as a child who couldn't stop telling stories, Nadia had always been vocal, envisioning futures bigger than her surroundings. As she grew older, she set her heart on opening an upscale nail salon redefining beauty and self-care. She pictured crystal chandeliers, plush chairs, flawless manicures that whispered luxury.

She spoke about it constantly—at family gatherings, on social media, and at casual meetups. She described every detail with passionate flair. At first, her excitement was contagious, drawing people in and making them believe in her dream. But as time passed, the weight of her words became chains. The more she talked, the more people expected immediate results.

"When is it opening?" they asked.

"Why isn't it ready yet?"

"Are you sure this is going to work?"

Nadia felt trapped by her own announcements. She spent energy explaining delays instead of resolving them, defending her vision instead of refining it. In a rush to meet expectations she'd created with her own words, she cut corners, hired cheap labor, and compromised on quality. The dream's original grandeur faded into a rushed, inconsistent reality that didn't satisfy her clients—or herself.

The noise she created had turned against her. She felt exhausted, discouraged, and ashamed. Her constant talking had built a pressure cooker, and her dream was burning inside it.

2. Leon: The Quiet Strategist

Leon grew up a few streets away from Nadia, but while others shouted their ambitions to the wind, Leon learned early that silence was often safer. He had a vision of building a tech startup that would serve communities often ignored by mainstream platforms. But he didn't announce it to the world. He kept his idea close, nurturing it in the quiet hours before dawn, coding, researching, and strategizing.

When people ask, "What are you up to?" Leon would smile and say, "Just handling some things." He didn't seek praise for steps not yet taken. He understood that words could scatter his focus, invite skepticism, or pressure him into premature moves.

In silence, Leon could think deeply, work steadily, and shield his dream from prying eyes. By the time he launched his first app, people were astonished at his accomplishment. "We had no idea," they said.

Leon simply shrugged. He didn't need them to know before it was real. His silence had been his secret weapon, allowing him to build without interference.

The Moment of Truth

A year later, Nadia and Leon crossed paths at a networking event. The room hummed with conversations, business cards exchanged, and promises made. Nadia arrived feeling worn out and battle-scarred. Her salon existed, but not as the sanctuary of luxury she had imagined. She felt the heavy burden of her words—the noise that had rushed her into poorly laid foundations.

Leon stepped into the event quietly. He had recently gained traction with his app, attracting investors and loyal users. He moved with a calm confidence, unruffled by the chaos around him.

Nadia approached him. "I wish I had your focus," she said softly, tears threatening at the edges of her voice. She envied his calm aura, the quiet certainty he carried.

Leon looked at her with understanding. "It's not focus—it's silence," he said, voice gentle. "When you stop explaining, you free yourself to act. Silence is where power grows."

Nadia realized then that her incessant talking had drained her power while Leon's silence had preserved and amplified his.

The Voice of the Source

Later that night, Nadia sat alone in her small apartment, surrounded by reminders of the dream she'd rushed. Broken equipment, inconsistent branding, and unhappy clients. She clenched her fists, feeling regret wash over her.

Then, the voice came—steady, unwavering:

"Nadia, why do you talk so much? Why do you announce your every move, defend your every thought, and seek their approval? Don't you see? The noise is your prison. The silence is your key." The voice struck a chord in her heart.

"You think talking makes you strong, but it makes you vulnerable. You think noise proves your worth, but it weakens you. Silence is where strength is born. It is where focus sharpens, plans grow, and power becomes unstoppable."

Nadia's tears dried. She saw how her words had given others power over her timeline, her process, her self-esteem.

"The world doesn't need your announcements—it needs your results. Move in silence, and let your actions roar. Stop explaining yourself to those who doubt you. Stop defending yourself to those who do not matter. Stop draining your energy on noise. Silence is your fortress. Build it, and nothing can break you."

The Law of Silence

"A quiet mind is a fortress. A quiet move is a checkmate. Stop talking. Start building."

Nadia understood now that silence wasn't emptiness—it was potential. It was the soil in which her dream could grow without disturbance.

How to Harness the Power of Silence

1. *Stop Explaining Yourself (Cut the Noise)*

    "Every explanation is energy lost. Protect your focus by withholding unnecessary words." Nadia realized she must save the energy wasted on justifications and pour it into her work.

    Action Step: Identify one area of your life where you explain or defend yourself too much.

    Commit to saying less and doing more.

2. Protect Your Plans (Move in Silence)

"Your plans are seeds. Expose them too early, and they may never grow."

Leon's success came from guarding his vision until it was ready to bloom.

Action Step: Write down your goals, but share them only with those who genuinely support you —or keep them private until you have tangible results.

3. Focus Your Energy (Act, Don't Announce)

"Every word you speak about your plans is energy diverted from building them."

By embracing silence, Nadia could channel her efforts into refining her salon, enhancing product quality, and delivering real value.

Action Step: For the next week, focus solely on taking action toward your goal without telling anyone about it.

4. Embrace the Power of Mystery (Let Results Speak)

"Mystery is strength. When no one sees your moves, no one can block them."

Leon's quiet achievements shocked skeptics and strengthened his position. Nadia could do the same by letting her improved services speak for themselves.

Action Step: Let your results, not your words, tell your story. Make silence your strategy.

Esoteric Insight: The Fortress of Silence

"Silence is not emptiness—it is strength. It is the space where power grows, where plans take shape, and where the world cannot interfere. A quiet mind is a fortress. A quiet move is unstoppable. Build your fortress, and the world will have no choice but to recognize your strength."

Nadia realized that in silence, she could reclaim control of her vision, free from the weight of external judgments and timelines. Silence became her shield, her sword, and her sanctuary.

The Final Word

The voice concluded:

*"Nadia, your words have been your chains. Your silence will be your liberation. Stop talking about the dream and start building it. Stop explaining your vision and start living it.

The question is not whether you can move in silence—you can. The question is: will you let go of the noise long enough to hear your own power?

The silence is waiting. Will you embrace it?"*

Nadia made her decision. She stepped back from the chatter, the justifications, the need to be understood. She invested her energy into refining her salon—choosing quality materials, hiring skilled workers, and perfecting customer experiences. Slowly, the improvements became evident, and clients noticed. Not because Nadia shouted from the rooftops, but because her work spoke for itself.

Now it's your turn.

Where are you creating noise instead of power? The time for talking is over. The time for silence has begun.

The question is: *Will you keep explaining yourself, or will you move in silence and let your actions roar?*

CHAPTER 13

The Phoenix Principle Burn to Rise, Break to Become

The Voice of Truth

Failure. Heartbreak. Loss.

They feel like death. They strip you bare, crush your spirit, and leave you with nothing but ash in your hands. The world tells you to avoid the fire, fear the burn, and run from destruction. But hear this truth: destruction is not the end but the beginning.

A phoenix cannot rise without first being consumed by flames. Creation demands destruction. Growth requires the breaking of what no longer serves you. You cannot rise until you've burned.

The fall is the lesson. The rise is the reward. The ashes are your foundation. The question is: will you let the fire destroy you, or will you rise from it stronger, sharper, and unbreakable?

The Story: Kenenan's Fall From Grace

Kenenan Martin had a basketball in his hand before he learned to write his name. Growing up on the outskirts of Houston, he spent countless hours on rundown courts, perfecting his crossover under flickering streetlights. He believed each drop of sweat, blister, and bruise would one day pave his way to the NBA.

By twenty-four, his dream felt closer than ever. A semi-pro standout, Kenenan caught the eye of an

Italian league known for scouting future NBA talent. The contract overseas felt like destiny. In Italy, he was welcomed like a rising star—fans chanted his name, sports journalists praised his explosive style, and local kids mimicked his moves.

Kenenan's Instagram and TikTok accounts blew up almost overnight. Videos of his games were paired with hashtags like:

#KenenanTheKing #DunkGod #Houston2Italy

But as his fame soared on the court, so did his reputation off it. Kenenan's nightlife adventures were as famous as his highlights, and he reveled in the attention without considering the cost.

The Social Media Hype

In Italy, Kenenan embraced the spotlight, curating a lifestyle that shouted, "I've made it." He posted endlessly: strolling through Milan in designer outfits captioned "Big Drip in the Big City 🌍

#FashionKilla #InternationalFlex," popping bottles in VIP sections after wins—"Celebrating another win the only way we know how 🍾🥂 #WinningLife," and going live at afterparties at 3 a.m., joking

"Who needs sleep when you're already living the dream? #NoDaysOff."

His followers ate it up, millions tuning in to see a young man who appeared to have everything: skill, style, and swagger. He believed the hype himself, thinking talent alone would protect him from consequences. But not everyone watching was impressed. Some observed with critical eyes, wondering if he valued stardom over substance.

The Million-Dollar Mistake

Unbeknownst to Kenenan, a major shoe brand had been scouting him, preparing to offer a seven-figure endorsement deal. This could have catapulted him from a rising athlete to a global icon. But before they signed, the executives reviewed his social media more closely.

They saw the late-night streams where he was clearly intoxicated, laughing about skipping practice. They noticed the Instagram stories showing him gambling with teammates before games. They cringed at the TikTok clip where he mocked another player's skills, boasting, "They can't touch me, even hungover."

This behavior clashed with the brand's image. They wanted a disciplined athlete, not a wild card. So they pulled the deal.

When Kenenan's agent broke the news, the words stung like a slap: "They can't back someone who doesn't take their career seriously."

Almost instantly, fans turned. The hashtags that once praised him transformed into ridicule:

"Bro, you were supposed to be focused on the grind. Smh."

"Imagine fumbling a bag like that 💀 #KenenanTheClown"

"You can't party your way to greatness, my guy. #LosingLife"

The opportunity slipped through his fingers. Instead of celebrating an endorsement, he was grappling with public humiliation and doubt.

The Ashes

The fallout weighed on him daily. His confidence wavered, his game suffered, and the once-loyal fans grew silent. Coaches benched him more often, frustration etched in their faces. Alone in his apartment, Kenenan scrolled through spiteful comments, each one cutting deeper than any physical injury.

"I messed it all up," he admitted, voice trembling in the quiet darkness. The dream he'd carried since childhood lay in ruins, and the ashes felt heavy in his hands. He wondered if he could ever recover, or if he'd burned his future beyond repair.

The Awakening

In that silence, stripped of applause and validation, a voice rose within him—not loud but unshakably clear:

"Kenenan, the fire you feel is not your end. It is your beginning. You cannot rise until you have burned."

He held his breath. The voice continued:

"You let distractions seduce you; the applause blind you. But the ashes of your failure are the foundation of your transformation. From them, you will rise—not as who you were, but as who you are meant to be."

Understanding dawned. His downfall wasn't a punishment but a purging of arrogance and carelessness, revealing what truly mattered—discipline, humility, focus.

The Phoenix Principle

"You cannot rise until you've burned. The fall is the lesson. The rise is the reward."

He realized that fire wasn't his enemy. It was the catalyst that burned away illusions, leaving him with a chance to rebuild himself stronger.

The Climb Back

The next morning, he took action. He deleted his social media accounts to silence distractions. He refocused on the basics: early morning workouts, solitary drills under dim gym lights, and rewatching game footage to pinpoint every flaw.

He turned down party invitations and abandoned useless indulgences. Frustration became his fuel, anger transformed into determination. Slowly but surely, progress emerged. Coaches noticed his renewed dedication. Teammates respected his relentless hustle. His mind cleared, his game steadied, and inch by inch, he climbed his way back.

He wasn't chasing applause anymore—he was building himself into a player worthy of respect, from the inside out.

The Voice of the Source

One night, after a strenuous practice, he sat alone on the empty court's edge, sweat cooling on his skin.

The voice returned, calm and certain:

"Do you see it now, Kenenan? The fire did not destroy you. It revealed you. It burned away the distractions and arrogance, leaving only your truth. From the ashes, you rise."

He nodded, heart steady.

"The fire will come again—it always does. But now you know the truth: the fire is your forge. Each burn prepares you; each fall makes you stronger. You are the phoenix. And the phoenix always rises."

How to Rise From Your Ashes

1. *Accept the Burn (Embrace the Fire)*

"The fire is not your death—it is your rebirth."

He accepted responsibility for his downfall, understanding pain as a necessary spark of growth.

Action Step: Write down what in your life is burning away—habits, beliefs, distractions. Accept that this destruction fuels your rebirth.

2. *Learn the Lesson (Find the Wisdom in the Ashes)*

"The ashes hold the truth. Look closely."

He realized hype and fame meant nothing without discipline and respect.

Action Step: Reflect on a recent failure. What truth did it reveal about you? Write it down.

3. *Rebuild with Purpose (Start the Climb)*

"The climb back is slow, but every step is progress."

He moved forward deliberately, focusing on genuine improvement rather than image.

Action Step: Choose one small action today that helps rebuild what you lost, stronger and wiser.

4. **Trust the Cycle (Rise Again)**

"The phoenix rises, burns, and rises again. The cycle makes you unstoppable." He knew future setbacks would come, but they would only refine him further.

Action Step: When faced with a challenge, remind yourself: "This is not my end. This is my transformation."

Esoteric Insight: The Phoenix Always Rises

"The fire feels like death, but it is life. It strips away the false and leaves only your truth. From ashes, you rise anew—not as who you were, but who you were meant to be. The phoenix does not fear the fire because the fire is its ally. You are the phoenix. Rise."

Kenenan embraced the cycle. Each time the flames licked at his edges, they only sharpened him.

The Final Word

*"Kenenan, the fire will come again, but fear it no more. Each fall is a lesson. Each rise is a reward. The question is not whether you will burn—you will. The question is: will you rise from the ashes, or let them bury you?

The fire is your forge. The ashes are your foundation. The rise is your destiny. Rise, phoenix. Your time has come."*

Now it's your turn.

What has burned in your life? What ashes remain, waiting for transformation?

The time for fear is over. The time for rising has begun.

The question is: *Will you stay in the ashes, or will you rise?*

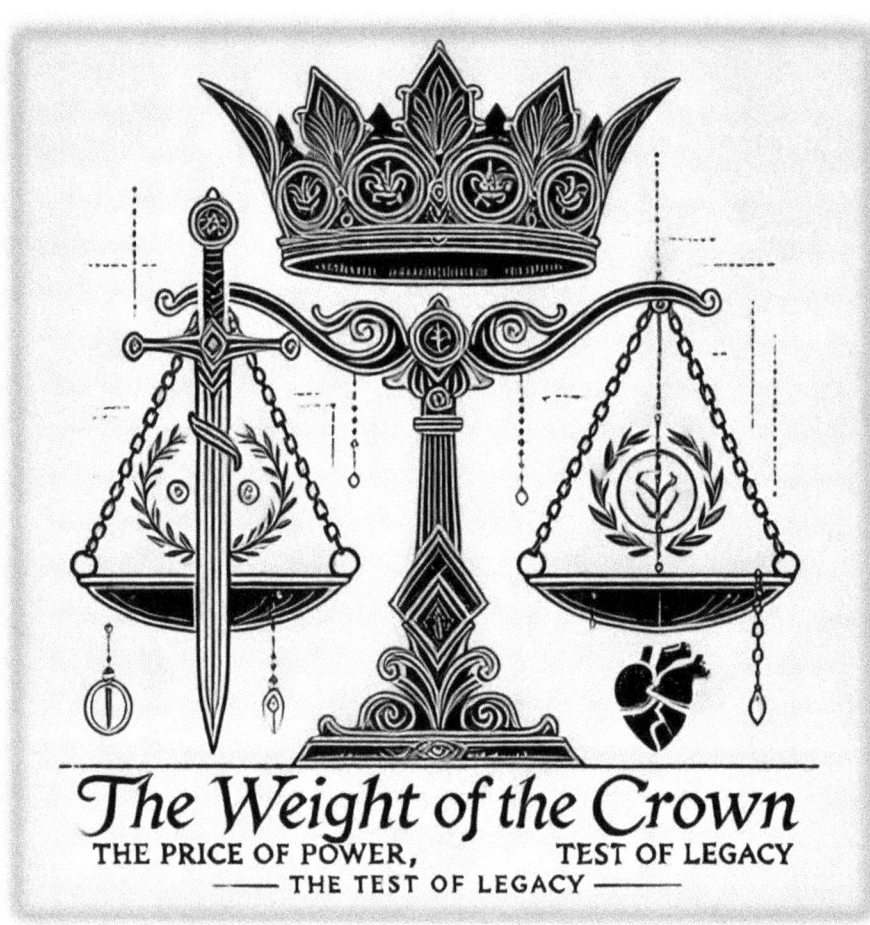

CHAPTER 14

The Weight of the Crown The Price of Power, The Test of Legacy

The Voice of Truth

Power is not given; it is earned. But what they don't tell you is this: power is heavy.

To wear the crown is to bear the weight of expectations, the burden of responsibility, and the eyes of the world scrutinizing your every move. The crown may shine, but it also presses down, testing your strength, your resolve, and your spirit.

Here's the truth: the crown is not for the faint of heart. It is for those willing to endure its weight, embrace its challenges, and rise under its pressure.

The question is not whether you can wear the crown—you can. The question is: will you break under its weight, or will you rise, unshakable, to build your legacy?

The Story: Sam and Ashley—The King and Queen

They met as kids in seventh grade, two bright sparks in a world that often felt too dim. Sam, even then, had an aura of confidence, a swagger that promised he would go far. Ashley, poised and cunningly intelligent, seemed born to lead. In the dusty halls of their middle school, they recognized kindred ambition.

By high school, they were inseparable. Sam rose as a football star, a quarterback who danced through defenses with flair. College recruiters circled. Ashley, meanwhile, was the orchestrator of events, the architect of class fundraisers, the voice at debate tournaments who never lost her cool. Together, they formed a rare synergy—each feeding off the other's drive and determination.

Their social media presence in those early days became a beacon. Sam posted game-winning touchdown highlights captioned: "Kings make moves, not excuses. 👑 #CrownMe" Ashley posted a valedictorian portrait stating: "Queens don't wait for the throne—they build it. 💎 #Legacy" Their combined hashtag, **#SamAndAsh**, trended locally every time they surfaced online. They were young, brilliant, and beloved. An entire community cheered for them, certain these two were destined for a dynasty.

The Rise

As predicted, after high school, their paths led upward. Sam earned a full ride to a top university, where he excelled on the field, his eyes always on the NFL. Ashley joined the same university on an academic scholarship, her analytical mind devouring opportunities and connections.

By their mid-twenties, the future they had once whispered about late at night was now tangible. Sam went pro, landing a coveted starting position as an NFL quarterback. Ashley channeled her organizational genius into an event-planning empire, attracting high-profile clients who trusted her flawless execution. Together, they branded their love and ambition as The Crown Collective—offering lifestyle coaching, motivational content, and exclusive merchandise.

Their lives dazzled. Lavish vacations in Bora Bora. Red carpet events with celebrities. Designer outfits, custom jewelry, and matching luxury cars. The captions told their story:

Sam: "It's not just a game—it's a kingdom. 🏈 👑 #KingEnergy"

Ashley: "Building empires isn't easy, but nothing worth having ever is. 💎 👸 #QueenMoves"

To the outside world, they were royalty, and their hashtag is still inspiring admiration—**#SamAndAsh**. But beneath the glittering surface, something heavy and unseen pressed down.

The Pressure of the Crown

Power had come at a cost. The crown they wore—this mantle of success, influence, and endless expectation—weighed more than either had foreseen.

For Sam, the NFL was a dream realized and a challenge unending. The grueling practices, the film sessions picking apart his every move, and the physical toll on his body tested him daily. The public demanded perfection. Fans expected wins; sponsors demanded results, and teammates relied on his leadership. Every misstep felt catastrophic. He carried it all on his broad shoulders, but sometimes at night, when he lay awake, he wondered if he could sustain this pace forever.

For Ashley, the empire they'd built was a testament to her skill. Her event-planning business dazzled clients, and The Crown Collective inspired countless followers. But the scrutiny was relentless. Every social media post received thousands of comments—some praising, some questioning, some tearing her down. She managed their public image, their brand partnerships, and their philanthropic ventures. The stress ate at her. Sometimes, she felt more like a curator of a museum displaying their perfect life than a human being living it.

They began to argue in private. Money, time, and the relentless grind—all sparked tensions. "You're never here, Sam," Ashley said one night, tears shimmering in her eyes. "The fans see you, but I don't."

Sam clenched his jaw. "And what about you? You're so busy managing our image that we've become just that—an image. Where's the love we started with?"

Their fights spilled over into their carefully crafted online personas. Fans noticed. Tabloids pounced:

"Cracks in the Crown? Sam and Ashley's Perfect Empire at Risk"

The Breaking Point

One particularly brutal night, after a heated argument, Ashley locked herself in their bedroom. She scrolled through old photos of them as teenagers—smiling, holding hands, no brand deals, no corporate partners, no crushing expectations. Just love and promise.

In the living room, Sam stared at the crown tattoo on his wrist. They'd gotten matching ink when their brand took off, a symbol of the power they claimed. Now, it felt like a cruel reminder of how far they'd drifted.

The silence was thick, charged with regret and longing. Then, the voice came—not loud, but unwavering:

The Voice of the Source

"Sam, Ashley, do you not see it? The crown you wear is not breaking you—it is shaping you. But you have forgotten its purpose. The crown is not meant to shine for the world; it is meant to remind you of your responsibility to each other, to yourselves, and to the legacy you are building."

The words wrapped around them, undeniable truth cutting through their pain:

"You think the weight of the crown is a curse, but it is your blessing. The pressure you feel is not here to destroy you but to forge you. The crown tests you because it knows what you are capable of. It is heavy because it carries your purpose. Will you break under its weight, or will you rise, unshakable, to prove your worthiness?"

They listened, hearts pounding.

"The crown is not for the faint of heart. It is for those who endure its trials, rise under pressure, and build something that will outlive them. The question is not whether you can wear the crown —you can. The question is: will you honor it?"

The Law of the Crown

"The crown is heavy because it carries your purpose. Rise under its weight, and you will build your legacy."

They realized they'd focused too much on appearances and not enough on the core of their bond, their mission, and their future. The crown's weight was a constant reminder that they had something precious to protect—not just their brand, but their love, integrity, and legacy.

How to Rise Under the Weight of the Crown

1. **Honor the Responsibility (Embrace the Weight)**

   "The crown is heavy because it matters. Honor its weight."

   Sam and Ashley understood they must approach their roles with respect rather than resentment. **Action Step:** Reflect on your responsibilities. Are you honoring them, or resenting them? Write down how you can approach them with renewed purpose.

2. **Strengthen Your Foundation (Build Together)**

   "A weak foundation cannot support a strong crown."

   They recommitted to communication, shared goals, and mutual understanding—remembering that their strength came from unity.

   Action Step: Identify one way you can strengthen your foundation—through honest conversation, quality time, or aligned visions.

3. **Protect Your Energy (Shield the Throne)**

   "Not everyone deserves access to the crown. Protect it."

   They set boundaries, limiting outside influence, filtering out noise, and safeguarding their mental well-being.

   Action Step: Write down what drains your energy. Create a plan to protect your focus from unnecessary distractions.

4. **Lead With Purpose (Focus on Legacy)**

   "The crown is not about power—it is about legacy."

They turned their gaze back to their long-term impact, using their platform to uplift others, inspire growth, and leave a lasting mark.

Action Step: Define your legacy. What do you want to build, and how will it outlive you?

Esoteric Insight: The Test of the Crown

"The crown is heavy because it is not just for you—it is for those who come after you. It carries your purpose, your trials, and your legacy. The question is not whether you can bear its weight—you can. The question is: will you honor it, or will you let it break you? The choice is yours."

Sam and Ashley realized their empire was more than a brand—it was a testament to perseverance, love, and ambition. The crown reminded them that their greatness wasn't measured by ease, but by how they responded under pressure.

The Final Word

The voice concluded:

*"Sam, Ashley, the crown is yours, but it is not for you alone. It is for the legacy you are building, the lives you are impacting, and the greatness you are called to embody.

The question is not whether you are worthy of the crown—you are.
The question is: will you rise under its weight, or will you let it fall? The crown is waiting. Will you honor it?"*

They made their choice. They let go of empty distractions, refocused on their partnership, and dedicated themselves to building a legacy grounded in truth and purpose.

Now it's your turn.

What crown are you carrying? What weight are you bearing? Power is heavy, but it is yours to hold if you honor it.

***The question is:** Will you break under the weight, or will you rise and build your legacy?*

CHAPTER 15

Legacy Over Ego Build Forever, Not for Applause

The Voice of Eternity

Listen closely.

The world has lied to you.

It told you that your worth is measured in likes, that your success is sealed by applause, and that your power is proven by the recognition of others. It taught you that clout is currency and validation the ultimate prize.

But hear this truth: ego fades. Legacy endures.

The applause you chase will fade into echoes long gone. The fame you seek will wither under the slow passing of years. The likes, the followers, the fleeting admiration of strangers—these are but shadows, illusions that slip through your fingers the moment you try to hold them.

Your name is not built on applause—it is built on what you leave behind.

This is the eternal truth: The world does not remember the loudest voice. It remembers the deepest impact. Those who build not for themselves but for others; who plant seeds in the soil of eternity, knowing they may never see the fruit. They understand that legacy is not a moment of attention, but a lifetime of contribution.

The question is not whether you will be remembered. The question is: what will they remember you for?

The Illusion of Ego

Ego is a thief.

It whispers that you must be seen, heard, praised to matter. It urges you to chase the spotlight, even when it blinds you. It prods you to climb a ladder of vanity, even when it leads nowhere. It demands approval, no matter the cost to your values.

But ego builds nothing that endures. It is the applause that quiets after the show ends. It is the fame that dissipates when the crowd finds a new idol. It is the shallow adoration of onlookers who vanish the moment you stumble.

You were never meant to live for ego's empty promises. You were not born to impress the moment.

You were born to shape the future.

The Path to Legacy

Legacy is built in silence, far from the roar of crowds. It is crafted in hours of quiet work, in the sacrifices you make when no one is watching, in the impact you have when no one is applauding.

Legacy does not need announcements. It does not beg for validation. It does not depend on the number of people watching—it depends on the depth of what you create, the lives you touch, the changes you spark.

The path to legacy demands patience, discipline, and unwavering commitment to purpose. It is the road less traveled because it asks you to think beyond yourself, to act not for applause but for meaning.

It may be lonely at times, carrying your vision through the darkness. But remember: seeds do not sprout under the glare of lights; they grow in the quiet darkness of the soil. Your legacy grows the same way, nourished by consistent effort, deep values, and sincere intention.

The Voice of Eternity

"Why do you chase what fades?"

The words cut through your mind like a blade.

"Why do you measure yourself by the applause of others, when their hands will one day grow still? Why do you crave the validation of the crowd, when their voices will one day go silent?"

The voice grows insistent:

"Do you not see it? The fame you chase is a mirage. The likes you gather are hollow. The approval you seek is a chain binding you to a life of emptiness.

You were not born to be a moment. You were born to be a monument. Stop chasing what fades. Stop seeking applause. Stop building for now—start building for forever."

The voice softens yet grows unyielding:

"Your legacy is not in how loud you are. It is in how deeply you shape the world. Your name is not built in likes—it is built in lives changed. The question is not if you will leave a mark; you will. The question is: will your mark fade with time, or stand as a testament to your truth?"

The Eternal Truth: Ego vs. Legacy

Ego is loud; legacy is quiet.

Ego demands recognition; legacy demands purpose.

Ego fades; legacy endures.

The choice is yours.

The Three Pillars of Legacy

1. Purpose Over Applause

"Clout fades. Purpose remains."

Ego says: "Look at me."

Legacy says: "Remember what I've done."

Action Step: Write down your purpose. What do you truly want to create, contribute, or change in the world? Let this purpose guide you instead of seeking applause.

2. Contribution Over Consumption

"You were not born to take—you were born to give."

Ego says: "What can I gain?"

Legacy says: "What can I give?"

Action Step: Identify one way you can contribute to others—through your time, skills, or resources. Focus on building others up, not just collecting praise.

3. **Integrity Over Popularity**

   "Fame is fleeting. Integrity is forever."

   Ego says: "Do what's easy."

   Legacy says: "Do what's right."

   Action Step: Reflect on your recent choices. Are they aligned with your core values, or shaped by a desire for approval? Commit to choosing integrity over instant gratification.

The Voice of Eternity: The Call to Greatness

*"You were not born for applause. You were born for greatness. Stop chasing what fades. Start building what endures.

The world will not remember your likes, your followers, or your fame. It will remember how you made others feel, how you changed lives, and how you left the world better than you found it. Ego is easy. Legacy is hard. But only one will outlive you. Choose wisely."*

The Legacy Mindset

- Build for others, not for yourself.
- Create with eternity in mind, not the moment.
- Let your actions speak louder than your words.

When you feel the pull of ego, remember that the applause will die out, the spotlight will dim, and the trophies will gather dust. But the seeds you plant in others—the knowledge you share, the kindness you show, the innovations you leave behind—these are the roots of your legacy. They will grow long after you are gone, keeping your spirit alive in the lives you've touched.

Esoteric Insight: Eternity Awaits

"Ego is a shadow, fleeting and insubstantial. Legacy is a light, eternal and unshakable. Build your light. Let it shine long after your time on this earth has passed. The question is not whether you can leave a legacy—you can. The question is: will you?"

This is your invitation to transcend vanity and embrace depth. To move beyond the empty thrill of recognition into the meaningful silence of lasting impact.

The Final Word

The voice concludes:

*"The time for chasing clout is over. The time for building forever has begun. Your legacy is waiting.

The question is not whether you will be remembered. The question is: what will they remember you for?

Will they remember you as a moment, or will they remember you as a monument? The choice is yours.

Build wisely. Build boldly. Build forever."*

As you step forward, choose legacy over ego. Plant seeds that will grow in fields you may never see. Let your work speak for itself, and let it echo across generations, shaping a future you may never witness but will always influence.

Now it's your turn.

Will you chase applause that fades with the night, or build a legacy that stands for eternity?

WHY I WROTE THIS BOOK

I wrote this book because I've been where you are.

I know what it's like to carry the weight of expectations, to feel the pull of dreams that seem too big for the life you're living. I know what it's like to fall, to fail, to lose everything and wonder if you'll ever rise again.

I wrote this book because I've walked through the fire. I've faced the storms that threatened to drown me and the shadows that whispered lies into my soul. And I've learned one unshakable truth: you are more powerful than you know.

This isn't just a book—it's a blueprint. A weapon. A guide to remind you of who you are when the world tries to make you forget.

- *It is here, in these final moments of our journey together, that I must reaffirm the purpose behind these pages. You have witnessed transformation, fought through inner battles, and discovered an immovable truth: greatness lives inside you. I wrote this book not to give you something you do not possess, but to help you recognize what has always been yours. This text is the key that unlocks a door in your soul, revealing infinite potential. It is a blaze that refuses to be dimmed by doubt. Remember, these lessons are drawn not from theory but from the crucible of experience— my own and countless others who dared to rise. This is not an ending, but a continuation of an ancient legacy, passed from one victor to the next.*

The Weight of the Crown Power is heavy.

The crown you're reaching for isn't just a symbol—it's a test. It's not just about leading others or building something great. It's about leading yourself, carrying the weight of your purpose, and rising under the pressure that tries to break you.

To wear the crown is to walk a path of responsibility, of sacrifice, of discipline. It's to wake up every day knowing that your actions ripple beyond yourself, that the life you live is a reflection of the legacy you're building.

Some people will look at the crown and see glory. They'll envy the shine, the attention, the admiration.

But they won't see the pressure it puts on your soul, the sleepless nights, the moments of doubt.

And that's why the crown isn't for everyone. But it's for you.

You're here because you've chosen to rise under its weight. You've chosen to embrace the pressure, to transform it into power, and to build something that will outlast you.

- *In a world where many shrink from the burden of greatness, you have chosen the more difficult road. The crown you seek is not handed out as a trinket of vanity; it is earned through sweat, tears, and unwavering resolve. As you step into the halls of history, know that the crown does not merely rest on your head—it fuses with your character, forging you into a guardian of time-honored truths. This crown demands growth, not complacency, and in accepting it, you set yourself apart from the countless souls who shy away from their destiny. Let these words echo through centuries: you have proven worthy, and the weight you carry will only increase your strength.*

The Power of Your Legacy

Ego fades, but legacy endures.

You weren't born to chase clout, to live for likes, or to perform for an audience that doesn't truly see you. You were born to leave a mark so deep, so undeniable, that it reverberates through generations. Legacy isn't built in applause. It's built in the lives you touch, the values you uphold, and the truths you live.

The world may not always recognize your greatness while you're here. It may not celebrate you in the moment. But true greatness doesn't need immediate validation. True greatness knows its worth lies in the seeds it plants, the foundations it builds, and the light it leaves behind.

- *Picture centuries from now, your name spoken in reverence by those who harvest the fruits of the seeds you sow today. Imagine entire movements sparked by your courage, entire communities uplifted by your vision. Legacy is a towering oak grown from a single acorn, nurtured by quiet sacrifices and unseen acts of compassion. Your legacy is the gift you offer to tomorrow, an inheritance for souls you will never meet. In your every action lies the power to shape destiny, to become a guiding star that future travelers use to navigate uncharted worlds.*

The Journey Forward

When you close this book, the real work begins.

This isn't the end of your journey—it's the beginning. Everything you've read and learned is only as powerful as the action you take.

The time for waiting is over. The time for doubting is done. The time to apologize for your power has passed.

Now is the time to rise.

Rise above the distractions that try to pull you from your purpose. Rise above the fears that whisper you're not enough. Rise above the systems that were never built to see you win.

You are the architect of your destiny, the master of your fate, and the author of your story. Every choice you make from this moment on is a brick in the empire you're building.

So build boldly. Build deliberately. Build with the knowledge that your legacy isn't just about you— it's about the lives you're called to impact, the truths you're called to speak, and the world you're called to change.

- *Imagine your path now, not as a straight line, but as a grand tapestry you weave with threads of wisdom and courage. Each decision you make is a stroke of paint on history's canvas, vibrant and enduring. Embrace the storms ahead, for they will sharpen your character. Embrace the challenges, for they will elevate your greatness. Let each setback be a stepping stone to greater triumph, each obstacle a test that reveals the depth of your resolve. With every step forward, you declare to the universe that you will not be denied your place among the legends.*

The Voice of Eternity

"Why do you hesitate?"

The words rise within you, not as a question but as a challenge.

"Why do you doubt your power? Why do you play small, when you were born to stand tall? The crown is not beyond your reach—it is waiting for you to claim it. But you must choose it. You must embrace the weight, the responsibility, the sacrifice." The voice grows stronger:

"This is your time. The world will not wait for you to feel ready. The world will not hand you your greatness. But you don't need permission. You don't need validation. You don't need anyone to crown you, because the crown has been yours all along."

- *Hear the voice resonate like a drum in your chest, each beat reminding you that you were never meant to linger in the shadows of uncertainty. The crown is not a distant star—it's a birthright waiting in your hands. The stage is set, the world is watching, and fate has dared you to claim what is rightfully yours. Feel the surge of electric possibility coursing through your veins as you realize all that's required is your unwavering decision. Let the roar of eternity fill your heart:*
  You stand on the precipice of greatness, and all that's left is to leap.

As you step forward, carry these truths with you:

Your power is in your actions, not your words. Speak less, build more.

Your worth is in your purpose, not their applause. Stop seeking validation. Start living your truth.

Your legacy is in your impact, not your ego. Build for forever, not for fame.

Remember, the journey won't be easy. The road will test you. The fire will come again. But every challenge is an opportunity to rise, to grow, to prove to yourself and the world that you are unshakable.

You are the king. You are the queen. You are the one the world has been waiting for.

- *Take these commandments as sacred oaths etched into your soul. Let them guide your every endeavor. Let them be the wind that fills your sails as you chart new territories of influence and inspiration. When doubt creeps near, recall these lines like a mantra. When fear tries to bind you, remember that greatness never belonged to the timid. You are royalty of the highest order, destined to shape the course of history, to become a beacon for all who dare to dream.*

The Final Word Thank you.

Thank you for walking this path with me. Thank you for trusting me with your time, your attention, and your belief in yourself.

This book was written for you—not to tell you who you are, but to remind you of what you've always known. You are greatness waiting to be unleashed.

Now go. Go and build your empire. Go and create a legacy that will stand the test of time. Go and prove to yourself that the crown you carry is not too heavy—it is perfectly fitted for you.

The question is not whether you will rise. The question is: how high will you soar?

Bryan.

Code name: Genesis.

Out.

- *And so we conclude, not with a whisper but a triumphant roar. Consider the power now resting in your hands—power to shape fates, ignite revolutions of thought, and lift countless souls through your example. Let the wisdom of these chapters echo in your mind and guide your steps. Remember, you hold within you the might to influence millions, to carve your name into the annals of eternity. History awaits your masterpiece. The world awaits your indelible mark. Fly higher than you ever imagined, and may your legacy blaze through the ages, forever illuminating the path for dreamers yet to come.*

www.ingramcontent.com/pod-product-compliance
Lightning Source LLC
Chambersburg PA
CBHW050528170426
43201CB00013B/2124